The
Little
Windows
Book

3.1 EDITION

Kay Yarborough Nelson

Peachpit Press
Berkeley, California

The Little Windows Book
3.1 Edition
Kay Yarborough Nelson

Peachpit Press, Inc.
2414 Sixth St.
Berkeley, CA 94710
(510) 548-4393

Cover design: Ted Mader + Associates (TMA)

ISBN 0-938151-81-9

0 9 8 7 6 5 4 3 2 1
Printed and bound in the United States of America

Contents

If you'd have my Advice, I'll give
it to you in short,
for a Word to the Wise is enough,
and many Words
won't fill a Bushel.

Benjamin Franklin, introduction
to *Poor Richard's Almanack*, 1758

Introduction

Windows 3.1 makes doing Windows easier. And this *Little* book makes learning how to use Windows easier, too. It's designed to give you just what you need to know to use Windows productively in a hurry. And it's got neat tips in it, too, that are way beyond the beginning level. So amaze your friends. Spend your lunch hour with this little book and see what you can do with Windows.

What's new in Windows 3.1? Basically, version 3.1 takes away a lot of the gripes and growls we made about Windows 3.0. It's a kinder, gentler version of Windows, and it's faster, too. For one thing, the Program Manager and File Manager have been streamlined and simplified. For another, support for TrueType fonts has been added, which gives you the benefits of using PostScript fonts without having to buy an expensive PostScript printer or purchase a font-management package. In addition, new "drag and drop" capabilities have been added: you can just drag an icon and release it on top of a program icon to start the program and open the document at the same time, or you can drag it to a minimized Print Manager icon to print it. If you've used Windows before, you'll realize what improvements these features are. (And if you aren't familiar with Windows, you soon will be.)

What's New?

What else? Lots. Some windows have status bars now that let you see what an icon's going to do if you double-click on it. There's a better button bar in Help, and Help has been revamped to make it more useful and less cumbersome.

What Else?

Behind the scenes, Windows has doubled the capacity of its system resources. A new StartUp group makes automatically starting programs as soon as you start Windows a breeze. Redesigned, more colorful icons improve the look of your desktop. New sound and multimedia capabilities have been added. And, in the "less is more" department, you'll get lots fewer of the dread UAEs—Unrecoverable Application Errors—that halt your work dead in its tracks. You can just press Ctrl+Alt+Del to exit from an unruly application without having to restart your system.

OLE, Too Object Linking and Embedding (OLE) in Windows 3.1 lets you create "objects"—icons that represent information from another program and put them in your documents. When you double-click on the embedded object, you can edit the spreadsheet or graphic or whatever just as through you were in the other program—which, in fact, you are. Not all Windows programs can do this yet, but you can expect to see lots of new programs and revised versions of existing programs that will make use of this capability.

And Multimedia... In the multimedia department, Windows 3.1 adds sound capabilities to your computer, if you have the right hardware, such as a sound card and speakers. A media player lets you play animation and sound files.

This is just a short preview of what the new Windows has to offer! You didn't buy this book to read an introduction, so on with the show.

A Guided Tour

If you've never done Windows before, this is the place to start. The short sections in this chapter introduce you to the basics of the Windows interface—what you see on the screen, and how you can interact with it.

What Can You Do with Windows?

Windows shields you from the ugly realities of your computer's operating system (DOS) with a graphical user interface that's a lot easier to use than DOS itself. (At least it's easier when you get used to it.) Windows also lets you run several programs at once, each in its own window, as long as you have a computer with enough memory. To switch between programs, you just click with a pointing device called a mouse.

Windows also lets you instantly transfer data from one program to another, so you can put text typed in your word processing program in your spreadsheet program, and vice versa. This is a feature your friends with Macintoshes have been bragging about for a long time now.

Windows and Non-Windows Programs

Windows runs all kinds of programs. Sure, it runs programs that were specifically designed for it, such as Microsoft Word for Windows and Excel for Windows, but it will also run other programs, like Lotus 1-2-3 Release 2.2 and DOS WordPerfect 5.1.

Get a Mouse!

A mouse is a pointing device that controls the position of the pointer on the screen. It's ideally suited for many tasks and pretty poor at others. What's it good for? It's good for

selecting large areas of text, for starting programs by clicking on their icons (those little pictures on the screen), for changing the position of windows on the screen, scrolling through text, and so forth. It's not so good when you're typing to have to take your hands off the keyboard and reach for the mouse.

Yes, you can run Windows without a mouse. But it's tedious. If you don't have a mouse, get one. You won't get the most out of Windows without one. You can get either a bus mouse (one that requires a card inside your computer) or a serial mouse (one that attaches to one of the communication ports on the back of your computer). Either kind comes with instructions for all you need to know to install it. Windows figures out what kind of mouse you have during installation, and it doesn't really matter to it what kind you have. If you haven't got one yet, you'll probably want to ask for a serial mouse, unless you like taking your computer apart and looking at its innards.

Windows has keyboard equivalents for just about everything you can do, but you're really crippled without a mouse. Enough said.

The Tour Begins

If you haven't got Windows started, you may want to start it now so that you can try out some basic techniques during this guided tour. If you've never used a mouse before, it takes some getting used to.

If Windows doesn't come up automatically on your computer, you can start it by typing *win* at the DOS prompt, which will probably be C:\> but may be D:\> or E:\>, depending on your computer.

You'll see the Windows desktop when Windows starts. The Program Manager is usually the first thing you see. Your screen may look a little different from the one shown here, if you or anybody else has previously used Windows on the computer you're using.

On the desktop, you can organize your work much as you would stack papers and move objects on a real desktop at home or at work. Small pictorial icons represent programs, groups of programs, documents, and desk accessories like a calendar or notepad. This desktop is sort of like the Macintosh's famous desktop, but quite a few of its features are different from the Mac's.

Calendar

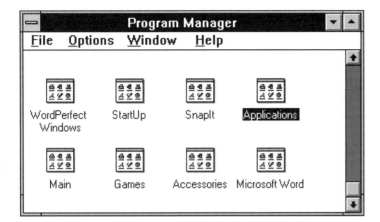

The mouse pointer is the small solid arrowhead on the screen. As you move the mouse on your real desktop, you'll see the pointer moving on the screen. Try it.

Here's the mouse secret: *you can pick it up.* If you've pushed the mouse all the way to the far corner of your (real) desktop and you're just about to knock over your cup of coffee but what you want is just a little farther over on the screen...pick up the mouse and move it nearer to you. The pointer will stay on the screen where you left it. Try it and see.

You use the mouse in three basic ways: by clicking, double-clicking, and dragging.

Using a Mouse

▶ **Tip:** *You can pick the mouse up! The pointer won't move.*

To select an item on the screen, you can move the mouse pointer to it and click once with the left mouse button. (If you're left-handed, you can change it to the right mouse button, as you'll see in the chapter on customizing Windows.) Selecting an item makes it active, so that you can work with it. For example, you might click on a document's icon so that you could copy or move it.

Clicking

▶ **Tip:** *You have to select something before you can work with it.*

You can also double-click on an item to make it active and actually start it.

Double-Clicking

▶ **Tip:** *Double-click on an icon to open it*

To double-click, quickly click twice with the left mouse button. For example, double-clicking on a program's icon will open a window and start the program.

Try opening the Program Manager's Accessories group by double-clicking on its icon.

▶ **Tip:** *The Object Packager lets you create live links between cut-and-pasted data in different programs.*

The Accessories group contains handy utility programs: Windows Write (a simple word processing program), a calendar, a calculator, a painting program, a character map, a sound recorder, and so forth.

Most of these accessory programs are relatively easy and fun to use, so you can explore them on your own when you feel more comfortable with Windows basics.

Dragging

A third way of using the mouse is dragging. To drag, put the mouse pointer on what you want to drag, press and hold the left mouse button down, and then move the mouse.

▶ **Tip:** *To move an icon to another place in the window, drag it.*

Try dragging one of the Accessories program icons and see how easily you can move it to different places inside the window. Release the mouse button when the icon is where you want it.

Dragging a window's border is also a way to resize the window and move it around on the screen. If you need to make your Accessories group window larger, try dragging one of its borders outward. You'll see the mouse pointer change shape when it touches the border.

Try opening another window so that you can see what's inside. Double-click on Windows Write, for instance.

Window Basics

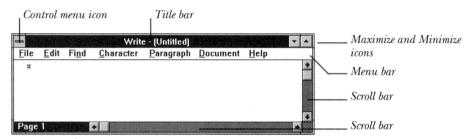

Control menu icon   *Title bar*

Maximize and Minimize icons

Menu bar

Scroll bar

Scroll bar

The title bar at the top of each window indicates which program is running in the window. Here, "Write - [Untitled]" indicates Windows Write. Untitled just means that you haven't saved any document yet. You can tell which window is active because its title bar is solid.

Only one window can be active at a time.

The Active Window

▶ **Tip:** *When a window is active, its title bar is solid.*

Just beneath the title bar, you see a menu bar. If you click on one of the menu items with the mouse, you'll see a pull-down menu. (You can also press Alt and type the letter that's underlined on the menu choice instead of clicking with the mouse.) If you click on File, you'll see the File menu.

Once you've displayed a pull-down menu, you can make additional selections from it by dragging the mouse down to the item you want and then releasing the mouse button. Or you can type the underlined letter.

Try choosing About Write... from the Write Help menu. Click on Help, keep the mouse button down, drag the mouse down to About Write..., and release the button. When you're through reading what it says, click OK.

Menu Bars

What you see is called a dialog box. A dialog box will appear whenever you select a pull-down menu item that has an ellipsis (...) next to it. If you choose Open... from the File menu, for example, you'll see a dialog box asking which file to open.

Dialog boxes let you supply additional information that the program needs. This one's asking which group you want to move a program to. (You'll see what that's all about later.)

Dialog Boxes

They can also give you information, like the About Write dialog box, or warnings about what you're doing.

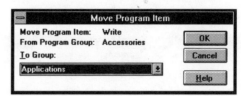

Click on OK in the About Write dialog box to close it and get it out of your way.

Scroll Bars Windows often can't display everything that's in a window at once. On the bottom and right sides of a window, you'll sometimes see a scroll bar. It indicates that there's more to the document than you can see on the screen. You can click in these scroll bars to move through your documents.

Since there's no document in your Write window, Windows will just beep at you if you try to scroll.

Windows that contain icons can also have scroll bars if there are so many icons that the window's too small to show them all.

Window Icons Icons can also represent small elements of a window. For example, the tiny icons in the upper-right corner of a window (the ones with the up and down arrowheads) are called the Minimize and Maximize icons. You use these to turn the document or program you're working on into a tiny icon and get it out of your way, or enlarge (maximize) it so that you can work in it again. Try this on the Write window.

▶ **Tip:** *Once you've minimized a window, double-click on its icon to enlarge it again.*

Another window icon is for a Control menu. It's the small box in the upper-left corner of the window, the one that looks like a tiny floppy disk drive. The Control menu will pop up when you click on that icon.

▶ **Tip:** *Closing a window removes the program from memory. Minimizing a window just makes it into an icon. The program's still in memory.*

A window's Control menu lets you move and resize windows and switch from one window to another. In most cases, there are easier ways to do what you want than to use them, such as using a keyboard shortcut or the mouse. You'll see lots of these techniques in the next chapter, where we'll look at working with windows in more detail.

To close the Write window so that you can get back to the Program Manager, click on Close.

The Program Manager

The Program Manager, as you've seen, is the program that automatically starts whenever you start Windows and continues to run in the background while you work. In fact, to exit from Windows, you exit from the Program Manager.

You use the Program Manager to start programs and also to arrange them into groups so that you can work with them more easily. For example, you might want to create a group of documents relating to one project, such as memo, letters, and budgets, along with your word processing and spreadsheet programs.

The Program Manager, when it first starts (that is, before you or anybody else starts using it), contains just a few group icons. A group icon looks like a tiny window with several small icons in it. You'll see how to create your own groups of programs later in the book.

Main

The Main group icon

The Program Manager's really in charge of running your programs, so before you go exploring on your own, here's a basic Windows secret, so that you won't get lost. You can always return to the Program Manager to find a program you're running or to exit from Windows.

▶ **Tip:** *You can always press Ctrl+Esc to get to the Task List and get back to the Program Manager.*

Task List

Tiffany Plus - 1-09.TIF
Program Manager
Dr. Watson
Clock - 2/10
WordPerfect - [Document1 - unmodified]

Switch To   End Task   Cancel
Cascade   Tile   Arrange Icons

USE END TASK TO DELETE DUPLICATE FILES IN THE TASK LIST.

It's easy to lose the Program Manager's window, though. Sometimes it can get hidden from view, especially if you have a lot of windows open on your desktop. Here's a trick for finding the Program Manager's window, in case you've lost it. Double-click on the desktop, outside any open windows. This brings up a special window called the Task List. See "Program Manager"? Double-click on it to go back to the Program Manager, or double-click on any of the other programs that you're running, to go to them. Click on Program Manager and then on End Task to exit from Windows.

Here's another common problem: You've opened so many groups that you can't see the Program Manager's window showing groups! You can use the Window menu to pick the next group you want, or choose Tile to get a peek into all the windows at once.

The Groups The Program Manager has only a few groups, until you add more: the Main group, the Accessories group, the StartUp group, and (yes!) the Games group. You've seen what's in the Accessories group already, but what about the others?

The Main Group Double-click on the Main group icon to open it. (If you haven't closed the Accessories group window and it's in your way, click its Minimize icon so that it will politely shrink away.) If you click just once on a group icon, you'll get the Control menu.

The Main group contains a set of programs that let you set up Windows, print, and manage your filing system, among other things. If your Main group window's not big enough to show them all, click on its Maximize icon.

- File Manager is a special program that lets you organize your files and directories. Because you can do so much with the File Manager, a whole chapter later in this book is devoted to it.

- Control Panel lets you set the colors of your desktop, install printers and fonts, and configure your system.

- Print Manager handles local and network printing.

- The Clipboard Viewer allows you to see what you've copied or cut from other programs.

- MS-DOS Prompt takes you out to the familiar C:\> prompt, where you can use the DOS command line.

- Windows Setup lets you install Windows programs as well as programs that weren't specifically designed to run under Windows but which will run anyway.

- PIF Editor is a utility you can use to set up non-Windows programs to run with Windows.

Click on the Minimize icon to shrink the Main group window back to an icon.

Windows and Non-Windows Applications Groups

When you installed Windows, you could choose whether you wanted Windows to search your hard disk for applications and create groups for them. If you did this, you'll also see a group icon for Applications in your Program Manager window.

Click on your Applications group icon to see what's in it. If you've purchased Windows programs like Word for Windows or Excel for Windows, you should see their icons when you open the group.

Games

Windows 3.1 even comes with a couple of games, Klotski and Solitaire. The object in Klotski is to move the red block out of the maze to an exit. In Solitaire, you're trying to build the four suits in order, just like in the card game. When you win, you get a great animated screen display. The Game menu in both programs lets you specify how some of their features work.

Solitaire

In Solitaire, double-click on aces to start your stacks; then double-click on cards to build the stacks.

In Klotski, keep the red block surrounded by small pieces; they're easier to move out of the way.

That's the fifty-cent tour of Windows basics, enough to get you started playing Klotski, at least. If you want to explore on your own, you can get more help by choosing Help from a window's menu bar. In the next chapter, you'll see more about working with Windows, including more about getting help.

Working with Windows

Windows has what's called a "rich interface." That's a fancy way of saying there are several zillion ways to do just about anything, either by using the mouse or by using the keyboard. This chapter tries to sort out some of the easiest ways to get basic tasks done, so that you can quickly get started using Windows. Later, when you're more comfortable with the program, you can explore other methods on your own. Like the stork theory, it won't quite cover all the details, but it'll do for now.

Just about the most basic skill you need in Windows is how to get help when you need it. To be able to get help efficiently, you'll need to know how to use menus, move around in a window, and use dialog boxes, so we'll look at those things first, in a little more detail than the quick tour in Chapter 1. Then we'll look at all sorts of ways you can arrange windows on your desktop.

You can get help on what you're doing in Windows by clicking on Help in the window's menu bar (pressing Alt+H will do it, too) or just by pressing the function key F1. Pressing F1 is the same as choosing Contents from the Help menu. It gets you the help index, where you can find help on this Windows program that you're running and Windows itself.

Need Help?

▶ **Tip:** *Pressing F1 gets you the Windows help contents.*

In fact, you can get help on using Help by just choosing How to Use Help from the Help menu! Here's the beginning of this Help window.

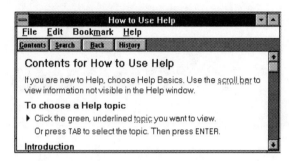

Once you've displayed the help system, you can get help in several different ways, Help has buttons called Contents, Search, Back, History, and glossary that let you jump around between topics. Clicking on the Back button will show the previous topic you looked up in the help system, so you can move through the system and branch to different topics.

If you click on the Search button, you'll see a list of key words and phrases. Type a word and press Enter or double-click on a listed topic. You'll see a list of related topics. Double-click on the topic you want to go to, or highlight it and click Go To to get a help screen on that topic.

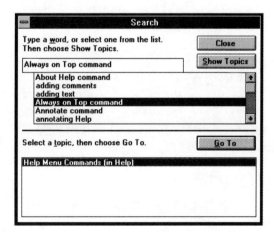

Another way to get help is to click on one of the words or phrases that are underlined, such as "Help Basics" in the first help screen. You'll immediately go to that topic. If you click on one of the words or phrases with a broken underline (like "scroll bar" in the figure), you'll get a pop-up window showing its definition.

You can also use the Help menu bar at the top of the screen, just as in any Windows program. (More on selecting from menus shortly.)

If there's more to the help screen than can fit in one window, you can scroll to see the rest of it.

▶ **Tip:** *Press Tab to move from one pop-up term to another in a Help window.*

Moving in a Window

Windows often can't display everything that's in a window at once. (This is almost always true of help windows.) On the bottom and right sides of a window that contains more than what's showing, you'll see a scroll bar. It indicates that there is more in the window than you can see on the screen. You can use these scroll bars to move through a document or text that's displayed in a window.

To move downward toward the end of the text, you can click in the lower part of the vertical scroll bar, or you can click on the small empty box in the scroll bar and drag it down. To move backward to the beginning of the text, click in the upper part of the scroll bar, or drag the empty box up. You can also move the mouse pointer to the boxes containing the up and down arrows, and press and hold the left mouse button down to scroll up or down.

A quick way to move through a long window is to click in the scroll bar at just about the place where you want to go. To go to the end of the window, click at the end of the scroll bar. Click in the middle to go to the middle. You get the idea.

▶ **Tip:** *Quick scrolling*

You can scroll horizontally by using the scroll bar and scroll boxes at the bottom of the window. These don't appear unless there's more in a window than what's showing on the screen.

Sometimes the keyboard's faster for scrolling than reaching for the mouse. If the window is displaying text, use the PgUp and PgDn keys. Press Ctrl-Home or Ctrl-End to go to the beginning or end of what's in the window.

Keyboard Shortcuts

Up to now, most of your practice has been with the mouse, but, as you just saw, you can also type at the keyboard. You may find that it's easier to use the mouse for making selections at first. Later, after you're used to Windows, you'll use the keyboard more.

Sometimes it's faster to use the mouse—to start a program by double-clicking on its icon, for example. But sometimes using keyboard shortcuts is faster, especially if you're typing along.

If a menu choice has a keyboard shortcut, you'll see it listed next to the item on the menu. On this menu, notice that just about everything has a keyboard shortcut!

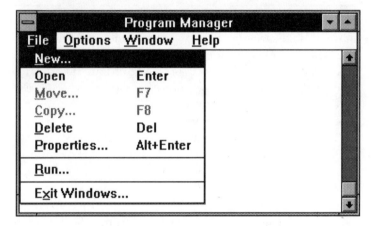

Windows has many keyboard shortcuts that you can use to speed up your work. After you work with Windows for a while, you'll probably memorize most of the shortcuts for what you do most often. A lot of them aren't on the menus, but you'll see what those are as we go along.

A big chart at the back of the book lists all the shortcuts and techniques, so if you need to look one up, you'll find them all in one place.

Selecting from Menus

Working with one Windows program is very similar to working with another, because you use the same basic methods for issuing commands, cutting and pasting, and switching from one program to another.

The menus you see on the menu bars depend on which program is running in the window. You'll get a File menu and an Edit menu in all Windows programs, but the rest of the menus may be different. If you're running Microsoft Excel, for example, the choices will be File, Edit, Gallery, Chart, Format, and so forth. In Microsoft Word they'll be File, Edit, View, Insert, and so on.

Remember from Chapter 1 that when you click on a menu choice in the menu bar (or press Alt and type the underlined letter), you'll get a pull-down menu.

You can select a choice from a pull-down menu by

- Clicking on it
- Typing the letter that's underlined (either lowercase or uppercase will do)
- Typing the shortcut key listed to the right of the option.

Sometimes combining keyboard shortcuts can save you several mouse operations. For example, pressing Alt+F and then typing O is a shortcut for selecting File from the menu bar and then choosing Open.

If a menu choice is gray, you can't select it. If there's a check mark next to it, it means that the choice is always either on or off, and it's on. (Selecting it again will turn it off.) If there's an arrowhead next to an item, selecting it will bring up another menu. If there's an ellipsis (...), selecting that choice will bring up a dialog box.

Using Dialog Boxes

Dialog boxes come up to ask for some other information that the program needs, or to verify that you really want to carry out a command. When you see a dialog box, you'll need to fill it out with the correct information (how you do this depends on what kind of a box it is) and then press Enter or click OK.

To move around in a dialog box, press Tab (Shift+Tab moves you backward) or just point and click with the mouse.

To back out of a dialog box without changing anything, just click Cancel, press Esc, or double-click in the Control icon to close the box.

▶ **Tip:** *Quick selecting: Type the underlined letter to go straight to a selection in a dialog box.*

15

List Boxes   You can scroll through list boxes with their scroll bars.
When you see what you want, click on it to highlight it. If
you don't have a mouse, you'll have to press Alt plus the
underlined letter of what you want to choose, and you'll
have to scroll with the PgDn and PgUp keys or the arrow
keys.

List box ———

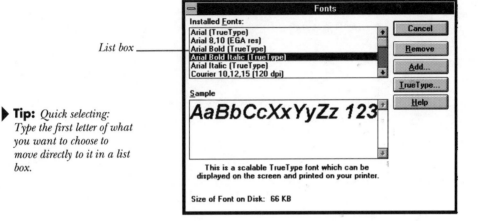

▶ **Tip:** *Quick selecting:
Type the first letter of what
you want to choose to
move directly to it in a list
box.*

Text boxes   If the dialog box is a text box, you'll need to type information the program needs. Here it's asking what you want to
find. First, click in the text box; then type the information.
The insertion point is indicated by an I-beam. You can use
the regular editing keys, like Backspace, to correct any errors you make as you type. You can also select text by
dragging over it.

Text box ———

Check box ———

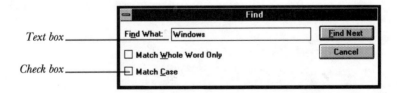

Check Boxes   You use check boxes to turn a feature off (not checked) or
on (checked). Click with the mouse to check or uncheck
something. Without a mouse, the space bar toggles the
check mark on and off.

Option buttons are round. Only one option button in a group can be selected. Click on the one you want to choose it. To deselect an option, click on another one.

Without a mouse, press Tab to get to the button you want. A dashed line will surround it when you can choose it. Then press the space bar to select it.

Command and Option Buttons

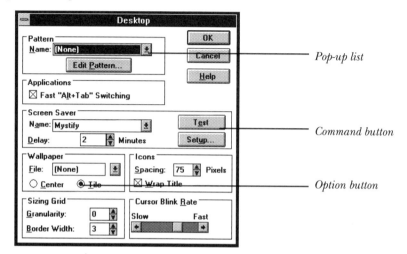

Pop-up list

Command button

Option button

Command buttons, like OK and Cancel, are square. If a command button has a bold outline around it, you can just press Enter to select it.

Sometimes you'll also see downward-pointing arrowheads (like the one next to None here) next to a text box. If you click on the arrow, you'll see a pop-up list that you can make additional choices from.

A set of up and down arrowheads indicates that you can change a setting by clicking on the arrows. Click the up arrow to increase the setting; click the down arrow to reduce it.

In some dialog boxes, you can just double-click on a button to choose it and close the dialog box with the OK button. This is one area in Windows where everything doesn't always work the same way, though. Try double-clicking to see if this will work in your dialog box.

Opening and Closing Windows

You'll be opening and closing windows a lot. The quickest way to open one is to double-click on its icon.

▶ **Tip:** *Press Alt-F4 to exit from an application, taking it out of memory.*

To close a window, you have several options. If you've got the mouse in your hand, the fastest way is just to double-click on the window's Control menu icon. If your hands are on the keyboard, pressing Ctrl+F4 is probably faster. You can also choose Close from the window's Control menu.

▶ **Tip:** *Double-clicking on a group window's Control icon turns the window into an icon.*

If you try to close the Program Manager's window, you'll get a dialog box asking if you want to leave Windows. Click cancel if you don't want to, or OK if you do. It's very easy to do this when what you really want to do is close the Accessories group window or the Main group window, for instance. This happens because there are really two different kinds of windows in Windows.

Application and Document Windows

There are basically two kinds of windows in Windows: application windows, which contain programs, like the Program Manager or the File Manager or Windows Write, and document windows, which are windows that belong to a program. *They don't necessarily hold documents!*

Document windows can also hold groups of programs, like the Program Manager's Accessories and Main groups.

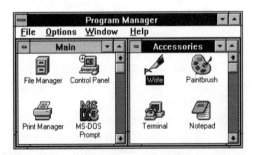

▶ **Tip:** *Application windows have menu bars.*

There's an easy way to tell the difference between an application window and a document window: an application window has a menu bar.

Most of the time, you never have to worry about which is which: you can just click in either kind of window to make it active. (The keyboard shortcuts are sometimes different for the different types of windows.)

In addition to clicking in the window you want to go to, there are other ways to move from window to window:

- You can display the Task List (by pressing Ctrl+Esc or by double-clicking on the desktop), highlight the name of the program you want to switch to, and choose Switch To (or just double-click on the program's name).

- You can press Alt+Tab to switch between the programs you've got running and the Program Manager, where you can start another program.

- You can press Alt+Esc until the window you want is active.

Moving between Windows

As you work with Windows, your screen can get cluttered very quickly. Here are a few basic techniques you can use to arrange the windows on your desktop so that you can see what's in them.

Arranging Windows and Icons

The easiest way to move a window is to drag it by its title bar. Click with the mouse in the title bar and, still holding the mouse button down, drag the window to where you want it.

You can move a dialog box, too, if it has a title bar: just drag it by the title bar. This is handy if a big dialog box is in the way of something you need to read on the screen.

The Control menu (the one under the little icon in the upper-left corner of the window) also has a Move command. You can choose Move and then press the arrow keys on the keyboard to move the window, pressing Enter when you've got it where you want it, but it's faster just to drag the window by its title bar.

Moving Windows

You may also want to make a window smaller or larger. Here again, this is a job for the mouse.

Move the mouse to one of the borders of the window. You'll see the pointer change shape to a two-headed arrow. When it changes shape, press the mouse button down and drag the window in the direction you want to go—outward to enlarge it, or inward to make it smaller. For example, to shrink it down to a smaller box in both directions, put the mouse pointer on one of the window's corners (it will change to the double arrowhead here, too) and drag it inward.

Resizing Windows

▶ **Tip:** *Quick sizing: drag the lower-right corner inward or outward.*

Yes, you can use the Control menu's Size command here too, (press the right arrow or left arrow keys until you've resized the window; then press Enter) but why bother? You move only one step at a time.

Maximizing and Minimizing Windows

The Maximize and Minimize icons in the upper-right corner of a window will shrink the window down to an icon or enlarge it to full-screen size. Minimizing a window when you're temporarily through working with it is a good idea because it keeps the screen from becoming too cluttered. You can just double-click on its icon to open it again.

Minimizing a help window with a lot of information in it that you're referring to back and forth is a good way to keep it handy.

Keep in mind that minimizing a window isn't the same as closing it! When you close a window, the program is removed from memory. When you minimize a window, it's still in memory, ready to use, just out of your way.

Click on this icon to restore a window to its former size

What if you maximize a window to full-screen size and then want to make it smaller? You can try and try to make the mouse pointer change to a double-headed arrow by moving it to a corner of the window, but it won't work! The trick here is to click on the Restore icon. It replaces the Maximize icon in the upper-right of the window when the window's full screen size. Clicking there restores the window to the size it was before you made it full-screen size. Subtle, huh? I had a hard time finding it.

Arranging Windows

If you don't want to arrange Windows by hand (or by mouse), you can use the program's built-in Tile and Cascade commands. They're on the Window menu and also on the Task List. If you choose Tile, the open windows will become smaller to fit across your desktop:

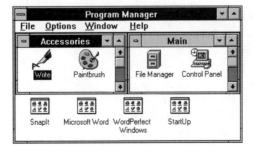

Choosing Cascade arranges the windows so that only their title bars are showing:

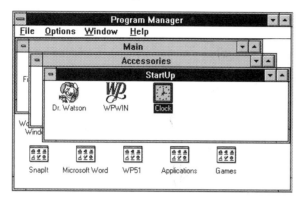

You'll find that tiling windows is useful if you're copying or cutting and pasting material between several different programs, because you can see more of what you're cutting or copying and where it's to go. Cascading is useful if you're working in only one window at a time but have several windows open and want to be able to see their title bars, so that you can remember what they are.

▶ **Tip:** *Tiling vs. cascading?*

The keyboard shortcuts are Shift-F4 for Tile and Shift-F5 for Cascade.

Even after you tile (or cascade) all your document windows, you may find that some windows are still hidden on your desktop. Here's the trick for cascading or tiling everything on the desktop: First, arrange all the application windows by bringing up the Task List (double-click on the desktop or press Ctrl-Esc) and choosing Cascade or Tile. Then choose Cascade or Tile from each application's Window menu (if it has one) to arrange all the document windows. (If you're running a non-Windows program, it won't have a Window menu.)

▶ **Tip:** *Find hidden windows by tiling (Shift-F4) or cascading (Shift-F5).*

Here's a hint: Once you've arranged windows as you'd like them, go to the Program Manager's Options menu and be sure that Save Settings on Exit is checked. That way, the next time you start Windows, your windows will be arranged the same way you left them.

▶ **Tip:** *Save your windows arrangement!*

Arranging Icons

Windows also has some built-in commands for arranging icons. You already saw how the Minimize box will shrink a window down to an icon. Well, the Task List and the Program Manager's Window menu both have an Arrange Icons command that will line up icons neatly. If your screen gets very cluttered, try it. (You'll see how to change the spacing between the icons in the chapter on customizing Windows.)

Moving Icons

▶ **Tip:** *Drag an icon to move it, or press Ctrl and drag it to copy it.*

▶ **Tip:** *Moving icons to the desktop*

Moving an icon in a window is easy. Just drag it to where you want it. You can even drag it into another group window. Press Ctrl when you drag if you want to make a copy of it. Windows 3.1 lets you move group icons into other windows to work with them. When you're done, they'll go back to the Program Manager window they came from.

You won't be allowed to drag an icon out of one of the Program Manager's groups and onto the desktop. To get an icon out on the desktop where it'll be handy for you to use, open it (double-click on it) and then minimize it.

In some windows, like the Control Panel, you can't move the icons at all. But you'll see that as you click on each icon, a message appears at the bottom of the window telling you what it's designed to let you do.

Quick Tips

On the next page is a quick rundown of the techniques you learned in this chapter, plus some of the (often obscure) keyboard shortcuts.

Get help	Click on Help on the menu bar, press Alt+H, or, press F1.
Move in a window	Drag or click in the scroll bars, or click on the arrow icons. In text windows, press PgUp or PgDn.
Select from menus	Click on the item or press Alt and type the underlined letter or number. When the pull-down menu appears, click on the item, or type the underlined letter or number. You can also highlight the name with the arrow keys and press Enter.
Move within a dialog box	Click in it, or press Tab to move forward or Shift+Tab to move backward.
Choose an item in a dialog box	Click on the selection, or type Alt+*letter* (where *letter* is the letter in the box).
Scroll a list dialog box	Click on the up or down arrow in the scroll box, or type Alt+*letter* and then press the down arrow key.
Open a window	Double-click on its icon or press Enter when its icon is highlighted.
Close a window	Double-click on its Control icon or press Ctrl+F4 .
Switch to a different window	Click in it, double-click on its name in the Task List, or press Alt+Tab to switch to the Program Manager and open another window there.
Move a window	Drag it by its title bar or use the Control menu's Move command.
Size a window	Drag it outward or inward by its corner, or use the Control menu's Size command.
Maximize a window	Click on its Maximize icon or choose Maximize from its Control menu.
Minimize a window	Click on its Minimize icon or choose Minimize from its Control menu.
Restore a window	Click on its Restore icon or choose Restore from its Control menu.
Tile windows	Choose Tile from the Windows menu or press Shift+F4.
Cascade windows	Choose Cascade from the Windows menu or press Shift+F5.

Working with Programs

All Windows programs have a few things in common, in addition to how you work with their windows. You start them all the same way, and once you're in them, you'll find similar menus in them. This chapter takes a look at some of the techniques Windows programs (and even non-Windows programs—those that aren't designed especially for Windows) have in common.

If you're like me, you want to get started working with programs right away, before you wade through a lot of details that you may never use about the Program Manager and File Manager. In fact, if you're really lucky and all the programs you'll be using are already in Program Manager groups, you may not need to use the Program Manager to create new groups until later, and you may not need to use the File Manager until quite a bit later, if at all.

The techniques in this chapter can get you started using the basics of Windows programs. If you see something you need more information about (like working with directories, for example) you can go to one of the other chapters to find out more about it.

Starting a Program

If the program you're starting is a Windows program, it will appear in a window. If it's not a Windows program, you'll probably first see it in a full screen when it starts.

If you have a 386 computer, you can press Alt+Enter to make a non-Windows program run in a smaller window. Pressing Alt+Enter again will return it to full-screen size.

You have several choices of ways to start a program running under Windows. Here are a few of them.

- If the program's part of a group, it's easiest to start the program in the Program Manager by double-clicking on the program's icon.

- If the program's not part of a group, you can use the Run command in either the Program Manager or the File Manager (it's on the File menu in both).

- You can go out to DOS by clicking on the DOS Prompt icon (in the Main group) and start the program running in DOS.

There are a couple of other ways you can start programs from the File Manager, but since they're a little tricky, we'll save them for that chapter.

Starting with the Program Manager

The easiest way to start a program is to double-click on its icon in the Program Manager. First, double-click on the group icon that contains the program you want to start; then double-click on the icon of the program you want to use.

▶ **Tip:** *Pressing Shift while you double-click will start the program and minimize it at the same time.*

If you've been working with Windows, you may have minimized the Program Manager's icon, or there may be so many windows open on your desktop that you can't find it. Double-click on the desktop (outside any windows or icons); then double-click on Program Manager in the Task List.

If you use a program often, you'll probably want to put it in a group so that you can start it by clicking on its icon in the Program Manager. You'll see how in the next chapter.

Starting with the Run Command

Programs that you hardly ever use can take up unwanted space in your Program Manager window. Instead of adding a little-used program to a group, you can start it by using the Program Manager's Run command.

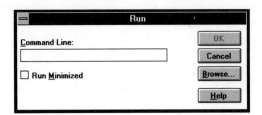

From the File menu, choose Run. Then enter the command you usually use to start the program from DOS and click OK (or just press Enter). For example, to start WordStar for Windows, enter *wswin*.

This works fine as long as the program is stored in the Windows directory, or if you've previously told DOS where it's stored by using the DOS PATH command. If not, you have to enter the program's path instead of just the command you use to start it. As far as Windows is concerned, path means "all of the directories that lead to the directory where the program is stored plus the command you use to run the program."

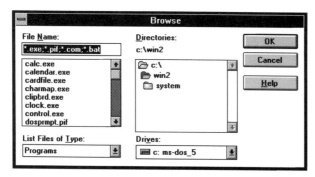

If you can't remember the command used to start the program, or if you don't know where the program's stored, click Browse. You'll see a list of all the program files in the current directory. To look in different directories, click on the folder icons until you find your program.

If this doesn't make sense to you yet, use one of the other ways to start the program until you read the File Manager chapter, where the mysteries of paths and directories and other DOS tricks will be explained.

If you don't want to work with the program immediately but would like it to be handy on your desktop, easy to find when you're ready to use it, click Run Minimized in the Run box. That will shrink it down to an icon and you can open it whenever you like by double-clicking on it. How tidy.

If you don't use the Run command, you can just click on the minimize icon to turn the program into an icon until you're ready to use it.

▶ **Tip:** *Click Run Minimized to keep your desktop neat.*

Starting with the File Manager

File Manager

You can also start a program by using the File Manager. (You'll see a lot more about the File Manager in Chapter 5.) Just double-click on the File Manager's icon, double-click on the directory the program is in (directories look like tiny folder icons) and then double-click on the program's name when the list of what's in the directory comes up.

How can you tell what's a program? Programs always have a .EXE or a .COM extension. Their icons look different from document icons or directory icons, too. They look like tiny windows with menu bars.

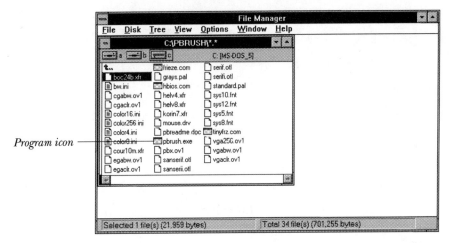

Program icon

You can also use the File Manager's File menu, choose the Run command, and then enter the command used to start the program you want to run, just like using the Program Manager's Run command.

Starting with a DOS Command

MS-DOS Prompt

Well, if you really want to use DOS... you can click on the DOS Prompt icon (it's in the Program Manager's Main group). That takes you out to the C:\> prompt, where you can start programs from the command line and work with them in DOS, without even knowing that Windows is there. When you're finished working in DOS, return to Windows by typing *exit* and pressing Enter.

If there's a program that you always want to start as soon as you start Windows, press Ctrl and drag its icon into your StartUp group icon (pressing Ctrl as you drag makes a copy of an icon instead of moving it). That way, the program will automatically start as soon as Windows starts.

You can do this with any of the accessories, too. For example, I put the clock in my StartUp group and have it run minimized so that it will always tell me the time when I look at my desktop.

Starting a Program When You Start Windows

Any Windows program you run will undoubtedly have File, Edit, and Help menus. This is part of Windows' "standard interface," so that once you understand how to do a common task, you don't have to learn it all over again in another program.

Using Windows Programs' Menus

You use the File menu for creating new files, saving them, and opening files you've already created. This one's for the File menu for Windows Write, but there are New, Open, Save, and Save As commands on all File menus.

Choose New whenever you want to start a brand-new, empty document. If a document's already on your screen, you'll get a chance to save it before Windows clears the screen to start the new document.

Choose Open when you want to open a document that's already been saved. You'll see a dialog box where you can click on the document you want to open. Use the scroll bars if the name of the document you want isn't displayed on the screen.

Creating Documents

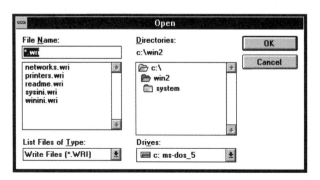

Windows will automatically display the contents of the current directory (this will usually be the Windows directory) and will automatically show you the files that normally belong to the program you're using. For example, if you're in Windows Write, you'll see all the files with a .WRI extension. If you're running the Notepad, you'll see all the files with a .TXT extension. The File Manager chapter has a chart that shows what all these extensions are and which programs they belong to, if you're interested.

To go directly to a document name in a long list, click in the box the list is in and then type the first letter of the name.

If you look through the whole list and don't see the document you're looking for, it isn't in the current directory. To see the list for another directory, click onanother folder icon. If you're not sure what directory the document you want is in, you can use the File Manager to find it, as you'll see later in the book. If you're not sure what a directory is in the first place... well, see the File Manager chapter.

Saving Documents Choose Save when you're ready to save your work. If you haven't saved the document before, you'll get the Save As dialog box, where you can enter a name and specify the directory where you want to store the saved file.

If you want to save the document you've been working on under another name, use the Save As command instead of Save.

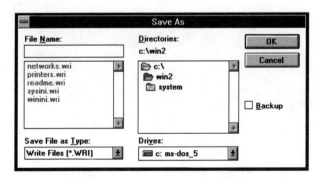

A few commands will also be common to all Edit menus, no matter what program you're using. For example, Windows provides an Undo command that miraculously undoes whatever you did last. (Alt+Backspace or Ctrl+Z is the keyboard shortcut for it.) You can restore text you deleted by mistake, change formats back to what they were before, and so forth. If what you did can't be undone, the Undo choice will be gray.

Editing Documents

```
┌─────────────────────────────────────────────────┐
│ ─         Write - [Untitled]              ▼  ▲   │
│ File  Edit  Find   Character  Paragraph  Document │
│ Help │ Undo Typing      Ctrl+Z │              ▲   │
│ this │ Cut             Ctrl+X  │                  │
│      │ Copy            Ctrl+C  │                  │
│      │ Paste           Ctrl+V  │                  │
│      │ Paste Special...        │                  │
│      │ Paste Link              │                  │
│      │                         │                  │
│      │ Links...                │                  │
│      │ Object                  │                  │
│      │ Insert Object...        │                  │
│      │                         │                  │
│      │ Move Picture            │                  │
│      │ Size Picture            │              ▼   │
│ Page 1    ◄ █                            ►       │
└─────────────────────────────────────────────────┘
```

Keep in mind that Windows only remembers the last thing you did, and that's all it can undo.

You'll also see Cut, Copy, and Paste commands on the Edit menu. As their names imply, you use them just as you would use scissors and glue to cut and paste material you've selected in the program you're working with. What's new about them in Windows is that when you cut or copy something, it also goes to a special area called the Clipboard, where it can be pasted into a completely different program from the one you're using.

When you cut text (or graphics), it doesn't really go away. Instead, it goes to the Clipboard. You can paste it into another place in your document, or into any other document, for that matter. You can even paste it into documents of other programs.

When you copy text, the copy goes to the Clipboard, too, so you can paste what you copy as well as what you cut. You can even copy between non-Windows programs.

The Clipboard

Clipboard
Viewer

▶ **Tip:** *Many Windows programs let you use the mnemonic shortcuts Ctrl+C, Ctrl+X, and Ctrl+V for Copy, Cut, and Paste. Some will even let you press Enter to copy selected text.*

To cut something, select it (usually by dragging over it to highlight it); then choose Cut from the Edit menu (or press Shift+Del or Ctrl+X). It will disappear from your document. At this point, it's on the Clipboard.

To copy something, use the same process: select it and then choose Copy (or press Ctrl+Ins or Ctrl+C). It stays in your document and a copy goes to the Clipboard.

To paste what you've cut or copied, put the insertion point where you want it to appear (just clicking with the mouse is easiest, but you can use the arrow keys, too). Remember, this can be somewhere else in the document (this is how you move text) or somewhere else in another document, or somewhere else in another program. Then choose Paste or press Shift+Ins or Ctrl+V. The contents of the Clipboard will appear.

If you're in a non-Windows program, the Paste and Copy commands (no Cut; sorry) will be on the Edit menu that you access from the Control menu. (Click on the Control icon in the upper-left corner of the window, or press Alt+Space bar; then choose Edit.)

▶ **Tip:** *If you're using a Windows program that supports OLE (Object Linking and Embedding), you can do a different kind of copying and pasting.*

To select something to copy, click on the window's Control icon and choose Mark from the Edit menu. You can use the mouse to select what you want to copy; when it's selected, just press Enter to copy it. To paste it in another non-Windows program, switch to that program and use the Control icon again, this time choosing Paste from the Edit menu. To paste it in a Windows program, use the regular Edit menu's Paste command or the shortcuts Shift+Ins or Ctrl+V.

See the "Oh, No!" chapter for more of these handy tips about working with non-Windows programs.

You can cut, copy, and paste text, data from a spreadsheet, graphics (although graphics won't always work if you're in a non-Windows program) results you've calculated with the Calculator, notes you've jotted in the Notepad—just about anything.

Once something's in the Clipboard, you can paste it over and over again; it doesn't go away until you cut or copy again.

You can be running the program in a window or full screen to do this, because when you press Alt+Spacebar, the Control icon will appear. To see if your non-Windows program will run in a window, press Alt+Enter while you're running it full screen.

Get used to the Clipboard; it can change the way you've been working up till now.

For example, you can use the Clipboard to save yourself a lot of typing time when a program asks you for information in dialog boxes. Suppose you want to find a certain phrase in Windows Write. Highlight the phrase and press Ctrl+C for Copy; then paste it in the Find dialog box instead of typing it again and maybe making a mistake.

To see what's on the Clipboard, double-click on its icon (it's in the Program Manager's Main group). What you copied or cut may not look just exactly as it did in the program, but it should be fine when you paste it in the other program. You can try choosing another format from the Display menu to see if it looks better that way.

Be careful: the next time you cut or copy, the data that was in the Clipboard will disappear, and the newly cut or copied data will take its place. Make sure you've pasted before you cut or copy again. If there's something in the Clipboard that you want to keep, you can save it as its own file by choosing Save As from the Clipboard's File menu (leave the .CLP extension if you want to use it again in the Clipboard). Once you've saved it, you can bring it back into the Clipboard by using the Open command.

Also, keep in mind that deleting and cutting aren't the same thing, not by a long shot. When you delete (with the Del or backspace keys), that material doesn't go to the Clipboard, and you can't get it back by pasting. Use the Undo command to get material you've deleted by mistake. Use the Paste command to paste what you just cut.

▶ **Tip:** *In Windows 3.1, there are new commands on a non-Windows program's Control menu that let you change its settings.*

▶ **Tip:** *Press Alt+Print Screen to copy the contents of a window. You can do this even if the window is full-screen size.*

▶ **Tip:** *Deleting and cutting aren't the same thing!*

Object Linking and Embedding

With Windows 3.1, you can embed "objects" in your applications. If you need to edit the object, all you have to do is simply double-click on its icon within your document, and Windows opens a window into the program that

Object
Packager

originally created it. For example, if you embed a Paint-brush drawing in Word 2.0, you're put back in Paintbrush when you double-click on the icon that represents the drawing, so you can use all the painting tools on it or change its fill pattern. If your Windows program supports this feature, you'll see an Insert menu.

You can embed an entire document in another document, even if the program that created the original document doesn't support OLE. But if you want to embed *part* of a document, both programs have to support it. To embed a whole document, go to the Object Packager and choose Import from the File menu. The select the document you want to import. From the Edit menu, choose Copy Package. Then open the document you want the embedded object to appear in and choose Paste Special from its Edit menu. You'll see an icon of the embedded object, and you can double-click on it to edit it in the program that created it. If Windows can't figure out which program that is, you'll need to associate that type of file with its parent program, and you'll see how to do that in Chapter 5.

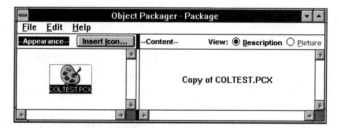

If you want to link the object instead of embedding it, choose Paste Link in your program. What's the difference? Linked data changes as you update it in the program that created it, but embedded objects give you more flexibility because you're able to access the original program instantly. Link when you need to share information with another file; embed when you need to edit and format that information back in the program that created it in the first place.

There are three basic ways to switch between programs:

- Click in the window that's running the program you want, or double-click on its icon on the desktop, if it's been minimized.

- Bring up the Task List (press Ctrl+Esc or double-click on the desktop) and double-click on the program's name. (Or you can choose Switch To, but that's just one extra step.)

- Press Alt+Esc to cycle among all the programs you've got running, including the Program Manager and any non-Windows programs. Stop when the program you want is active.

▶ **Tip:** *In Windows 3.1, you can press Alt+Tab to switch between your program and the Program Manager if you've checked Fast Alt+Tab Switching in the Desktop Control Panel.*

If you're running a non-Windows program in full-screen mode, when you press Alt+Esc, you'll see your program as an icon at the bottom of the screen.

Double-clicking on a program's icon on the desktop isn't the same as double-clicking on its icon in the one of Program Manager's windows. If an icon's out on the desktop, the program is really "open"—its window has been minimized—and double-clicking on it just opens it again. If you double-click on an icon in the Program Manager, you start a new copy of the program running, and it won't have the document you've been working with.

If the program you want to switch to hasn't been started yet, it won't be in a window. Here's a tip for starting it quickly (if it's part of a group). Bring up the Task List with Ctrl+Esc, double-click on the Program Manager, click on its Window menu, and click on the name of the group the program is in. You can then double-click on the program to start it. For example, to start the File Manager, press Ctrl+Esc, double-click on Program Manager, click on Window, double-click on Main Group, and (finally) double-click on the File Manager's icon.

When you're ready to leave Windows, you quit by exiting from the Program Manager. The fastest ways to do this are either to double-click on the Program Manager's Control icon in the upper-left corner of its window or press

Alt+F4 when the Program Manager's active.

Another quick way to exit Windows is to bring up the Task List, highlight the Program Manager's name, and click End Task. (You can also choose Exit Windows from the File menu, but the other ways are faster.)

If you try to leave Windows and there's a document you haven't saved yet in a program you're running, you'll get a chance to save it. So the absolutely fastest way to depart from Windows and quit from all the programs you've got running is just to go out to the Program Manager and quit Windows instead of closing all the programs one by one.

If you want to save the arrangement of the group windows and icons you were working with, make sure the Save Settings on Exit command in the Program Manager's Options menu is checked.

Here's a quick rundown of the techniques you've seen in this chapter.   **Quick Tips**

To	Do
Start a program	Double-click on its icon. Press Enter when the icon is highlighted. Choose Run from the Program Manager's or File Manager's File menu. Double-click on the DOS Prompt icon and use DOS.
Start a new document	Choose New from a File menu (or press Alt+F and type N).
Open a document	Choose Open from a File menu (or press Alt+F and type O).
Save a new document	Choose Save As from a File menu (or press Alt+F and type A).
Save a document	Choose Save from a File menu (or press Alt+F and type S)
Undo what you just did	Choose Undo from an Edit menu (or press Alt+Backspace).
Cut	Select; then choose Cut from an Edit menu (or press Shift+Del or Ctrl+X).
Copy	Select; then choose Copy from an Edit menu (or press Ctrl+Ins or Ctrl+C).
Paste	Select; then choose Paste from an Edit menu (or press Shift+Ins or Ctrl+V).
Copy the contents of the screen	Press Print Screen (or PrtSc).
See what's on the Clipboard	Double-click on its icon.
Delete a character	Press Backspace or Del.
Select a word	Double-click on it.
Select several lines	Click at the beginning, press Shift, and click at the end.
Switch between programs	Click in the program's window, or double-click on its icon, or choose Switch To from the Task List, or press Alt+Esc to cycle among all the programs that are running.
Leave Windows	Exit from the Program Manager (double-click on its Control icon or press Alt+F4).

The Program Manager

Central to Windows is the Program Manager. It comes up when you first start Windows, even if you've set up Windows so that something else will start, too. You use it to start programs and to exit Windows—in fact, you can't exit from the Program Manager without leaving Windows, too.

Besides running the whole show, the Program Manager is also a valuable tool that you can use to organize your work into groups of programs and documents that you use frequently. Once you've done that, you can easily find the icon representing what you need to work with, click a couple of times, and start working. No more "What was the name of that document?" and "Where did I save it?" or "What command do I use to start this program?"

As you saw briefly in Chapter 1, the Program Manager comes with several groups already set up for you, such as the Main group, the Accessories group, an Applications group, and the Games group.

The Program Manager

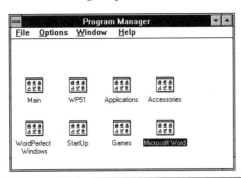

The Main group contains the File Manager, Control Panel, Print Manager, PIF Editor, Clipboard, DOS Prompt, and Windows Setup programs. (I've added a few more groups to my own Program Manager.) The File Manager, Control Panel, and the Print Manager are so important that they'll be discussed in separate chapters.

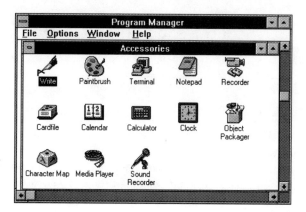

The Accessories are a standard or scientific calculator, a daily and monthly calendar with an alarm, a Rolodex-type cardfile, an analog or digital clock, an easy word processor called the Notepad, a fairly sophisticated painting and drawing program called Paintbrush, a Program Information File (PIF) editor for setting up information about non-Windows programs, a macro recorder, a communications program called Terminal, and Windows Write, a word processing program. Windows 3.1 has a few new accessories.

New Accessories Windows 3.1 adds a Character Map that lets you easily insert special symbols in documents, a Media Player for using animation and sound, and a built-in Sound Recorder that you can use if you have a sound recording or playback device attached to your system.

It also has a sophisticated Object Packager that lets you paste data or graphics into a document and keep in contact with the program that originally created it. For example, you might create an object that consists of data from a spreadsheet program into a word processing document. When you click on the icon that represents the object, you're immediately placed back in the spreadsheet program.

In addition to these groups, you may have an Applications group, if you let Windows set it up for you during installation.

More Groups

The Program Manager takes up a lot of real estate on your desktop. You can fix it so that it runs as an icon, out of your way when you're not using it. Choose Options from its menu bar; then choose Minimize on Use. When you start another program, the Program Manager will politely get out of your way.

Working with the Program Manager

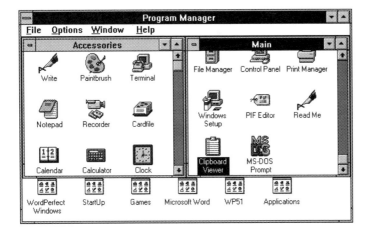

The Program Manager is just a little different from other Windows programs. For one thing, it has group icons and group windows. Group windows are the Program Manager's windows, like the Accessories and Main groups. They contain icons that, if you double-click on them, will start programs and open documents. Group icons are simply group windows that have been minimized.

The important thing to remember about group windows is that they don't close like other windows. In fact, they don't close at all: they become icons. If you double-click on a group window's Control menu to close it (or press Ctrl+F4, which is a keyboard shortcut), it will shrink down to an icon.

If you double-click on a group window's title bar, you'll maximize the window.

▶ **Tip:** *Neat trick: Double-click on an icon in a group; then minimize it to make it into an icon on the desktop.*

You can't move a group icon out to your desktop. If you try to drag it, it becomes a "No way!" symbol. If you want to get one of the programs that's in a group out to the desktop so that you can find it easily, double-click on it; then minimize it.

The Window Menu

The Program Manager has a handy Window menu that lists all the groups that have been created. (It's handy because it lets you switch between groups without having to cycle through all the opened windows on your desktop.) The active group will have a check mark next to its name. To make a different group active, just click on its name. This will also bring that group window to the front of the stack, so if you have a lot of windows open on your desktop, it's a neat trick for finding the group you're looking for.

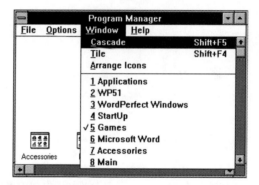

You can also press Ctrl+F6 or Ctrl+Tab to move from group to group within the Program Manager.

Creating Your Own Groups

You'll probably find that organizing programs and documents that you work with frequently into groups makes them easier to find and use. What kind of groups should you create? Well, that's up to you. You could keep your spreadsheet program in a group along with budgets you use often, or you could keep your word processing program in a group with the documents you work with most frequently, or you could organize your work by project and keep all the programs you work with daily and all the related documents you have to deal with in one group. Just because you put a program or a document into a group doesn't mean that you can't start the program or work with the document from somewhere other than the Program Manager. Not at all. In fact, you can start programs and open documents from the File Manager, or from the DOS prompt, just like always. Putting a program in a group just gives you a new way to start it.

To create a group of your own, choose New from the Program Manager's File menu. You might think this lets you start a new document, but it doesn't. Instead, you'll see the New Program Object dialog box.

Creating a New Group

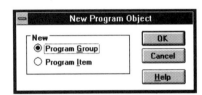

Click on the Program Group button, since you're creating a new program; then click OK (or just press Enter). You'll then see the Program Group Properties dialog box. Enter a description (remember, this description will appear on the screen). If you've been using DOS, you've had a lot of practice at writing short, pithy descriptions for file names. You don't have to be that terse here. You can even use whole words! And spaces! If your descriptions get so long that they overlap on the screen, just space your icons farther apart. See Chapter 6 for how.

Leave the Group File box blank (Windows will fill it out for you); just click OK when you're done with the description.

The group window you've created will be open. You can now add programs and documents to it.

Adding a Program to a Group

▶ **Tip:** *Drag to move; Ctrl-drag to copy.*

The easiest way to put a program in a group is just to move or copy its icon from another group.

To move a program icon to another group window, just drag it. To copy a program icon, press Ctrl and drag it. You can make a copy in the same group window, or in a different group window.

Here's a tip: If you use an accessory program like the Calculator or Calendar or Cardfile a lot, you can make it a part of a group. Just copy the icon into the group.

To delete a program icon, click on it to highlight it; then choose Delete from the File menu or press Del. You'll be asked to confirm that this is really what you want to do. Deleting a program icon doesn't remove the program from your hard disk! The only way to do that is to use the File Manager's Delete command, or the DOS DEL or ERAse commands.

▶ **Tip:** *Assign a shortcut key to a program you use often, so that you can switch to it by pressing that key combination.*

Another way to add a program to your new group is to choose New again from the Program Manager's File menu. This time, select Program Item from the New Program Object dialog box and click OK. (It may be already selected for you.) You'll see the Program Item Properties dialog box.

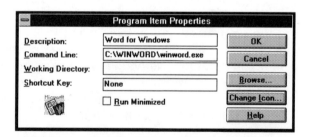

In the Description box, type the description you want to appear under the item's icon. If you're planning to include a document with this program item (more on that soon), it's a good idea to use the document's name as a part of the description. In the Command Line box, you'll need to put the information telling Windows where to find the program and what command to use to run it. There's an easy way to do this: click Browse to see all the executable (program) files in the current directory. Then just double-click on the name of the program you want to add, such as winword.exe for Word for Windows. Windows will add its path and the command that starts it to the Command Line box.

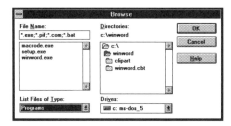

If the program you want to add isn't in the current directory, you can change directories by clicking on the folders in the Directories box.

Windows will automatically assign an icon to the program you've added to the group. Sometimes more than one icon is available for a program, especially if it's a non-Windows program that hasn't had an icon assigned to it. Click on Change Icon and View Next to see if you'd rather have a different icon for the program.

Adding a Document to a Group

If you want to include a document with a program, you can do that, too. Then, when you click on the program icon, you start the program and open the document at the same time.

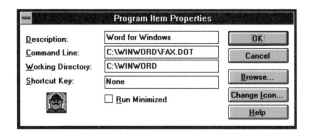

To include a document in a program icon, use the handy Browse button and click the pop-up list arrowhead under List Files of Type. Choose All Files and click on the document you want to be opened whenever you double-click on the icon. Windows will handily fill out the boxes for you.

Changing the Document's Icon

You can put several documents in a group, but only one document can be included with each program icon. There's a little problem: The program will be represented by the same icon, even if the icons are set up to open different documents. To be able to tell your icons apart, click Change Icon and then click Browse to hunt for other icon files you may have (they end in .ICO).

▶ **Tip:** *Seeing more icons.*

Here's a trick you can use to locate more icons: In the File name box, enter c:\windows\progman.exe; then click OK. You'll see lots of icons you can choose from!

Also, be sure to use a different descriptive name for each program-plus-a-document icon you set up so that you can tell which is which, like the Fax Man icon I set up that actually starts Word for Windows and opens a document template for a fax form.

Fax Man

There are lots of third-party Windows programs you can buy that have collections of ready-made icons like this one.

A small warning: When you start the program from its icon, you're in effect starting another copy of the program. It's possible that you could run out of memory if you start enough different copies of a large program. If that happens, you'll have to exit from a few of them (see the "Oh, No!" chapter for troubleshooting tips).

Adding Programs with Windows Setup

A quick way to add several programs to groups at the same time is to use the Windows Setup utility. You may want to do this if you've run out and bought a bunch of new Windows programs after installing Windows. Don't confuse it with the StartUp group. It's in the Program Manager's Main group.

Windows Setup

To start Windows Setup, double-click on its icon. You'll see a screen listing particulars about your hardware—what kind of display you're using, the keyboard and mouse you have, and so forth. Choose Set Up Applications from the Options menu.

You'll then see the Set Up Applications dialog box. Choose whether you want to search for applications or whether you want to specify one to set up. Click OK to start the search.

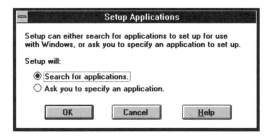

Windows will then ask you where you want it to search: your whole hard disk, or just in the directories listed in your path. (If you're not sure what a path is, stay tuned for Chapter 5.) it will the search, stopping occasionally to ask you about the names of programs it's found. When it's done, you'll see the programs it found listed on the left. Highlight any you want to make into Program Manager group icons (you can click on more than one, or choose Select All to select all of them) and then click OK. Windows will put them into the Applications group. You can move them into other groups later.

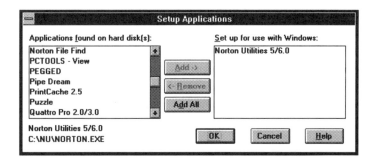

There's also a way to use the File Manager to put programs in groups. You'll see it in the File Manager chapter.

Changing a Group's Name

If you want to change a group's name, click its icon. Then choose File and then Properties. Type a new name and click OK. That's it.

Deleting a Group

▶ **Tip:** *Deleting an icon doesn't delete the program! It's still on your hard disk.*

At some point you'll probably decide that you'd like to get rid of some of your groups. To delete a group, click on its icon and then choose Delete from the Program Manager's File menu. You'll be asked to confirm that that's really what you want to do. You delete group icons and program item icons the same way.

Running Programs from the Program Manager

Here's a brief rundown of how to run programs from the Program Manager.

Double-click on an icon to start the program and open any document that you've included with it. (The program has to have been added to the group before you can start it.)

To start a program from the DOS prompt, click on the DOS Prompt icon (it's in the Main group) and then use the DOS command line as you normally would. This is a good way to start programs that you hardly ever use and don't want to bother making a part of a group. When you're done, type exit at the DOS prompt to return to Windows.

There's another way to have Windows open documents and start programs at the same time. You can associate documents that have the same extension with specific programs. You'll see how in the File Manager chapter.

Here's a quick rundown of the techniques you've seen in this chapter.

Quick Tips

To	Do
Shrink a group window to an icon	Double-click on its Control menu or click on its Minimize icon.
Maximize a group window	Double-click on its title bar or click on its Maximize icon.
Create a new group	Choose New from the Program Manager's File menu; click Program Group; fill out a description and a command line.
Add an item to a group	Copy or move the program's icon into the group (press Ctrl and drag to copy it; drag to move it). Or choose New from the Program Manager's File menu; click Program Item; fill out a description and a command line.
Change an item's icon	Click Change Icon in the Program Item Properties dialog box.
Add a document to a program item	Add the document's name to the end of the command line in the Program Item Properties dialog box.
Change a group's name	Click its icon; choose File and then Properties.
Delete a group	Click its icon and press Del.
Add a program via Setup	Double-click on the Setup icon; choose Options and then Set Up Applications.
Move a program icon to another group	Drag it.
Copy a program to another group icon	Press Ctrl and drag it.
Run a program from the Program Manager	Double-click on its icon.

The File Manager

The File Manager is Windows' utility for letting you do your computer "housekeeping"—moving files around, viewing what's stored on a disk, locating a particular file, and so forth, and version 3.1's File Manager is a big improvement over version 3.0's. In fact, Windows itself is a big improvement over the way DOS made you do these things. Instead of copying files by using cryptic commands, for example, you can just drag their icons.

We're not going to look at everything the File Manager can do, or you'd be in this chapter for the rest of the day! We'll just examine the things you'll probably do most often.

But before you begin to look at the File Manager, it's important that you understand at least a little bit of how DOS organizes your files behind the scenes. Windows does a pretty good job of keeping you away from DOS, but you still need some idea of how its system of files and directories works, so that you can *find things.*

If you're already familiar with files, directories, and paths, just skip to later in the chapter.

Each document you create and save is stored as a file. There are different kinds of files.

Program files have a .COM or .EXE after them, like windows.exe. (These three characters are called an *extension* because they're an addition to the file name. They can help identify what kind of file it is.) Files like these are executable programs. You can run the program, but you can't see what's inside the file.

Files and Directories

Document files can contain text, graphics, spreadsheet data, or what have you. These are the files you create by using programs. They may have all sorts of extensions, like .TXT for a Notepad file, .XLS for an Excel spreadsheet, or even no extension at all. WordPerfect, for example, doesn't use any extension.

There are also other files that certain programs need, like printer and system files. These, too, have all sorts of extensions. You usually can't see what's in them. If you see anything, it'll be garbage.

Naming Files   DOS (and therefore Windows) is pretty rigid when it comes to letting you name files. Unlike naming icons, where you can use whole words with spaces between them, you can only use eight characters for file names. (Plus that three-character extension, but most Windows programs will add that for you automatically.)

Forbidden Characters   There are some characters you can't ever use in file names:

<>	angle brackets
\	backslash
|	bar
[]	brackets (either one)
:	colon
,	comma
=	equals
+	plus sign
"	quotation mark
;	semicolon
/	slash

If you use a period, DOS will think it's the beginning of the extension, so be careful and only use a period there and nowhere else.

You can use some other symbols, though: $ ~ # @ ! ' ( ) { } - _ and ^ are all acceptable. They can help you give a more descriptive name to a file, such as 10-28LTR for a letter you wrote on October 28.

These are all acceptable file names:

BOB_2.WRI, SUE-1.TXT, LTR#3

These are not:

BOB/2.WRI, SUE+1.TXT, LTR*3

DOS converts everything to uppercase letters, so just type away in lowercase; it doesn't matter.

Popular Extensions

Windows automatically assigns extensions to many of the files you create, depending on which Windows program you're in. Here are some of these so that you can identify which program they belong to:

.BMP	Paintbrush graphic
.CAL	Calendar file
.CLP	Clipboard file
.CRD	Card file
.INI	Windows settings files
.MSP	Paintbrush graphic (older version)
.PCX	PC Paintbrush graphic
.PIF	Program Information File
.TXT	Notepad file
.WRI	Windows Write file

Here are some extensions other popular programs use:

.WKS	Lotus 1-2-3
.XLS	Excel
.WSD	WordStar
.DBF	dBASE

Naming Your Files

Using only eight characters to name all your files means that you've got to be pretty creative. The best thing to do is set up a system and follow it rigidly. For example, you might decide to name all your letter files like this, by date: 10-2LET. This would mean (to you) that the file is a business letter written on October 2. A letter written on November 13 would be 11-13LET.

You may not want to use the date, because you can use Windows to see the date the file was last changed (more on this later). Instead, you might organize files by project, or by client, or by type of file (report, budget, and so forth). As long as you use a consistent naming system, it'll be easy to locate the file you're looking for. But if you get sloppy and start naming a few documents TIM_LET or QUOTE, you've blown your system and may have trouble finding what you're looking for. Set up a system. Be consistent.

Directories   On your computer, files are organized into a system of directories. Think of a directory as a file folder in your filing cabinet. You can put all kinds of things in a directory—programs, different documents, graphics, whatever you like. Directories can even hold directories, which are called subdirectories, just as you stuff folders inside other folders in a filing cabinet.

The Root Directory   At the very beginning of your directory system is what DOS calls the root directory. All the directories and subdirectories branch off from it. Everybody says it's like a tree and its branches, but it's not: it's like an *upside-down* tree and its branches. The root is on top, folks. (This is somewhat typical of DOS thinking.)

When you start your computer and get that C:\> prompt, you're at the root directory. The C: indicates that you're on drive C, which is usually the name of your hard drive. It may be D: or E:, depending on your computer, but A: and B: are usually floppy disk drives. The \ indicates the root directory. That's why you can't use it in a file name.

If you've never ever created any directories before, all of your files will be in the root directory, except for your Windows files and maybe your DOS files. They'll be in directories named C:\WINDOWS and C:\DOS, which were created when you installed them. It's really much easier in the long run to use a more organized filing system. The File Manager can help you set yourself up a system of directories and subdirectories.

At the top of each directory listing in the File Manager will be a tiny arrow with two dots next to it. Clicking on this symbol will back you up one level of directories toward the root directory. If you keep clicking on it, you'll eventually wind up at the root directory.

The Path

At this point, you're probably wondering how DOS (and you) can keep track of where things are, if you've got subdirectories within subdirectories within subdirectories. Well, that's where the path comes in.

The path is just a list of all the directories that lead to the directory that contains the file that you're looking for, like the house that Jack built. What's confusing about the path is the cryptic notation you use to write it out. You separate each directory with a backslash, so C:\WINDOWS\WRITE is the path to a subdirectory named WRITE under the WINDOWS directory on drive C:.

When you use the File Manager, you can get a graphic representation of where your directories are and what's in them, so you won't have to worry about paths very often. But you do have to use them sometimes in the File Manager, so remember that you read about it here.

DOS is automatically told the path to your Windows directory when you install Windows.

Finally, the File Manager! But, believe me, you need to know the preceding stuff so you won't get lost.

The File Manager

File Manager

The File Manager is in the Main group, although you might expect that it would be right out there with the Program Manager. Well, the File Manager is a little different, and it works in just a little different way.... You'll see.

When you double-click on the filing cabinet icon, you'll see the File Manager's screen. It will be showing a window called the Tree on the left side of the screen, and all the files and subdirectories that are in the current directory will be displayed in a directory window on the right side of the screen. (Yours will look different, of course, since it will show the directories on your computer).

The path

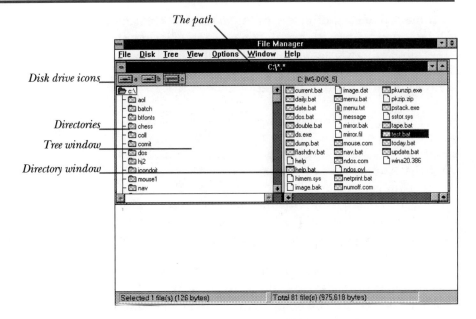

Disk drive icons

Directories

Tree window

Directory window

At the top of the screen, all the disk drives on your computer are represented by little drive icons. This one's got three: A: and B: are floppy disk drives, and C: is a hard drive. It's showing what's on the C: drive. (If you're on a network, you'll see slightly different icons for network drives.) To change to another drive, click on the icon for that drive. You'll see another set of windows showing what's on that drive.

▶ **Tip:** *Maximize the File Manager's window to see more files and directories.*

The C:\ next to the open folder under the drive icons indicates that you're looking at the root directory of drive C:. If you click on one of the directory folders, it will open and you'll see what's in it in a directory window on the right side of the screen. If a lot of files are in there, you'll have to scroll, probably both horizontally and vertically, to see them all. The title at the top of the window will change, showing you the path to the directory you're in. The notation will be just like you saw earlier when we talked about what a path was. Each directory name will be separated by a backslash.

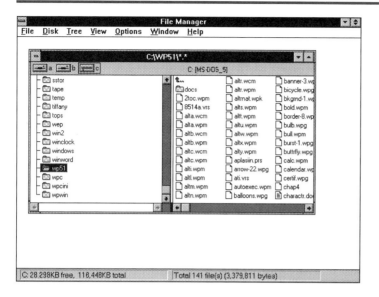

You can choose whether you're looking at the directory tree, just the files in the directory, or both. Click Tree on the View menu to see your directory structure.

Seeing the Directory Structure

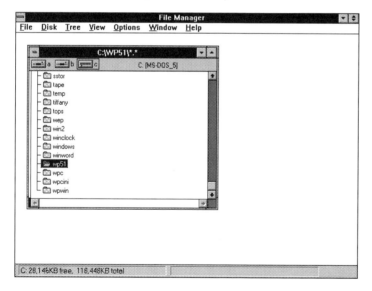

▶ **Tip:** *Typing an * (use the numeric keypad) is the shortcut for expanding a branch.*

If you want to see into the structure of your directory system, you can use the Tree menu. Highlight a directory and choose Expand Branch. You'll see any subdirectories that are in that branch.

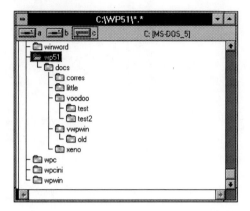

To see your whole directory structure, choose Expand All from the File Manager's Tree menu. You'll then see a graphical representation of how all of your directories are structured.

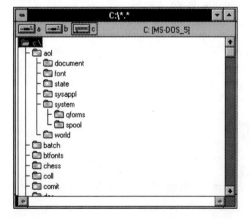

If you'd like an indication of which directories have other directory folders in them, choose Indicate Expandable Branches from the Tree menu. Directories that have subdirectories will then have a + on them.

A + means that a directory's collapsed. When it's expanded, it will have a - on it.

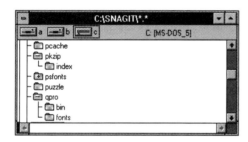

Here are a few shortcuts for expanding and collapsing directories. Press

Expanding and Collapsing Directories

+   To expand a selected directory one level (assuming it's got a + on it)

*   To expand all the selected directory's subdirectories

▶ **Tip:** *Use the *, -, and + keys on the numeric keypad.*

Ctrl- *   To expand all the subdirectories of all of the directories

–   To collapse the directory (assuming it's got a - on it)

You can use the Tree menu's Expand One Level, Expand Branch, Expand All, or Collapse Branch commands if you forget what these shortcuts are.

To collapse the whole directory display, just click on the root directory's icon (the one at the very top of the display) and choose Collapse Branch (or type a –).

Looking in a Directory Window

In a directory window, the files represented by the little icons with a bar across the top are program files. They look sort of like tiny windows with a menu bar. If you double-click on one of them, you'll start the program it represents.

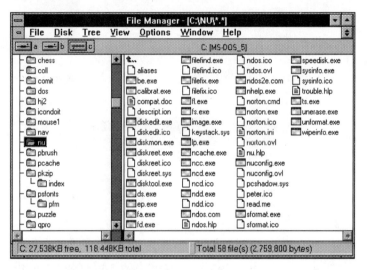

▶ **Tip:** *Use the View menu's Split command to resize Tree and directory windows. It will automatically show you both kinds of windows, too, if you're looking into just one kind.*

The files with the little icons with a bar across the top are program files. If you double-click on one of them, you'll start the program it represents.

Those that have lines across them are files that have been associated with a program. (You'll see how to associate files and programs later.) If you double-click on one of them, you'll start the program that it belongs to as well as open the document.

Those without lines that have one corner turned down are other files—dog-eared, as some people call them—are files that your program needs, or files that haven't been associated with a program yet. You'll just get an error message if you double-click on any of these icons.

To go up one level, double- click on the symbol with two dots and an arrow at the top of the listing (pressing Home will take you right to it).Depending on where you are in your directory structure, you may have to click on that little arrow more than once to reach the root directory. Once you're there, you can move down that branch.

The File Manager lets you open directory folders to your heart's content, but it only shows you what's in one folder at a time. You can open more than one directory at a time by choosing New Window from the Window menu. This will open a window looking into the same directory you were looking in before. You can tell because the title line will show the same path, followed by :2. You can click on other folders in that window to look in other directories, though.

Here's an easier way: Instead of choosing New Window to see into a specific directory, Shift-double-click on its folder. Then tile the windows by pressing Shift+F4 if you need to be abler to see into more than one at a time. (Being able to look into several windows at once is often handy when you're copying and moving files, as you'll see later.)

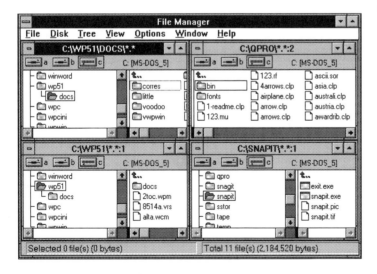

Climbing the Branches

Tip: *If there's a file you use frequently and always have to scroll to find, rename it with a number. That way, it will appear near the beginning of the directory listing.*

Tip: *To open a window into a different drive, just double-click on a drive icon.*

Tip: *Shift-double-click to open a new window..*

Minimize Windows

▶ **Tip:** *If you're planning to work with the File Manager again soon, don't close it. Just minimize it. It'll be easier to find later.*

If you find that you're using one directory window over and over, minimize it while you're not using it! It will appear out on the File Manager's screen, where you can get at it again easily by double-clicking on it. To minimize a directory window, click its Minimize icon.

Use the Window Menu

If you minimize a directory window, it won't go zipping out to the desktop like a group window will in the Program Manager. It will still be at the bottom of the File Manager's window, and you may have to move or resize some other File Manager windows to find it. A quicker way is to use the Window menu. It will list all the directory windows you've got open (minimized is still "open") and you can click on the name of the one you're looking for.

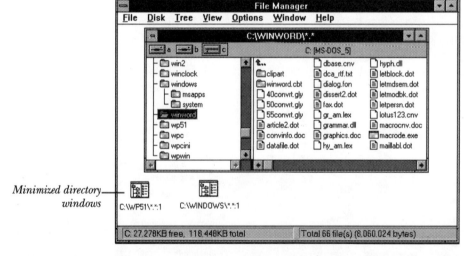

Minimized directory windows

Saving Settings

If you check the Save Settings on Exit command on the Options menu, all your directory windows will be arranged the same the next time you open the File Manager. So if you want to see into the sane directories you were looking into before, check this command.

The File Manager simplifies your work with routine file management chores like moving, copying, and renaming. But before you can move or copy files and directories, you'll need to select them. Usually, you just click on the one you want.

To select more than one file, if they're next to each other, use the Shift-click method: Click on the first one; then press Shift, hold it down, and click on the last one. If they're not next to each other, press Ctrl and click on each one.

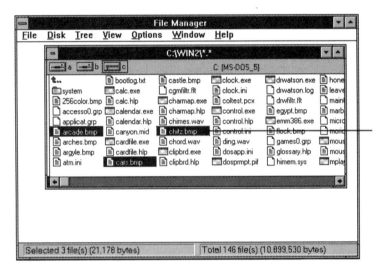

▶ **Tip:** *Ctrl-click or Shift-click to select several files.*

▶ **Tip:** *Quick selecting: Type the first letter of the file or directory's name to go straight to that part of the alphabet.*

Ctrl-click to select nonadjacent files

Selecting different groups of files is a little tricky, but here's how to do it. To select several groups of files, Shift-click to select the first group. The press Ctrl and click to select the first file in the second group. Then press Shift and Ctrl and click on the last file in the second group. Repeat Ctrl-click and Shift-click as needed to add groups. ways to use the keyboard. They work fine as shortcuts, but you wouldn't want to have to do this all the time!

You can use the File Manager's Select Files command if you want to use wildcards to select files. Wildcards are special characters that can specify a pattern for a group of files that have similar names or similar extensions, so that you don't have to type each file name individually. The

▶ **Tip:** *To deselect one file, press Ctrl and click on it. To deselect all but one file, click on that file.*

Using the Select Files Command

characters * and ? are called wildcard characters. Just like in poker, a wild card can stand for something else. The asterisk (*) represents any number of characters (including none at all), and the question mark (?) represents any one character.

For example, to copy everything ending in .XLS (Excel spreadsheets), enter *.XLS. To copy everything beginning with A and having any extension, like APRIL.WRI or AB_DOC.TXT or ACCOUNT.XLS, enter a*.*. To copy both the files BROWN.TXT and BRAUN.TXT, enter BR??N.TXT. Using wildcards can save you time, but they take a little getting used to.

Keyboard Shortcuts for Selecting and Deselecting

If you don't have a mouse, you'll go nuts when it comes to selecting and deselecting files. Here are a few ways to use the keyboard. The work fine as shortcuts, but you probably wouldn't want to have to use them all the time.

To	Press
Select a file	Type the first letter of its name to go to that part of the alphabetical listing
Select adjacent files	Shift-arrow keys (Mouse: Shift-click)
Select nonadjacent	Press and release Shift-F8; then use the arrow keys to move the selection box. Press the space bar to select. (Mouse: Ctrl-click)
Ctrl-/	Select all files
Ctrl-\	Deselect all but one file

Copy and Moving Files and Directories

You'll often want to copy files or move them to new locations. Windows definitely makes this easier than DOS did! To copy and move files and directories, you just drag them to where you want them. If they won't go where you want to put them, you'll be told.

First, arrange the screen display so that you can see both what you're copying and the window or icon of where you're copying it to. (Use the Shift-double-click trick to open the directory windows and then tile them.) Select the file you want to copy (for several files, Shift-click or Ctrl-click). If you're copying a whole directory, select its icon. If you're copying several directories, select their icons. Then drag the file or directory icons to their new destinations.

If you're copying them to new locations on the *same disk*, press Ctrl while you drag. (If you don't press Ctrl, you'll move the files instead of copying them.) If you're copying to a different disk—say, a floppy disk in drive A: —just drag.

You'll be asked to confirm what you're doing if there are duplicate file names already in the new location. If you copy a file on top of a file that has the same name, you'll overwrite what was in the old file.

A copied directory will be placed *under* the directory you dragged it to, and it will appear as a subdirectory.

If you're copying a lot of files into a lot of different directories, minimize the directories and then just drag the files onto the directory icons. This can save you a lot of window arranging.

▶ **Tip:** *Minimize directory icons for multiple copy jobs.*

To copy via the keyboard, use the Copy command on the File menu and fill out the From: and To: sections of the dialog box. Use the path for the To: destination, as it will undoubtedly be in a different directory!

If you highlight the file (or files) you want to copy first, they'll automatically be put in the From: box (it may not show them all, if you've selected a lot of them).

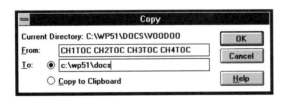

The advantage to using the Copy command instead of selecting icons and dragging them is that you can use wildcards to specify a lot of files at once.

You can also copy whole directories and all their contents by using the Copy command. Just enter the path to the directory, like C:\WINDOWS\BUDGETS, in the From box and enter the new destination in the To box.

Moving

Moving files and directories is just like copying them, except that they don't stay in the old location as well as appearing in the new location.

To move files and directories to new locations on the *same disk*, just drag them with the mouse. To move them to a different disk, press Alt while you drag.

Here's a reminder:

Drag	To copy onto a different disk
Drag	To move on the same disk
Ctrl-drag	To copy on the same disk
Alt-drag	To move onto a different disk

▶ **Tip:** *The keyboard shortcut for Move: F7.*

You can also use the Move command from the File menu if you want to use wildcards with a bunch of files to be moved.

If you move a directory, all of the files in it moves with it. Windows places the moved directory *under* the directory where you moved it.

Renaming Files and Directories

Easy. Select the file or directory and choose Rename from the File menu. Enter the new name in the dialog box and click OK. Just remember to follow DOS's rules. See "Naming Files" earlier in this chapter for a refresher.

Creating a New Directory

If your file system is a mess, you can use Windows to straighten it out. One of the first things you'll need to do is create some new directories so that you can organize your files in them.

Here's how to do it. Choose one of the Tree views from the View menu and click on the directory that you want the new directory to be created under. For example, you'd click on the WINDOWS directory to create a new subdirectory for it.

From the File menu, choose Create Directory. You'll see a dialog box where you can enter the name you want your new directory to have. Enter it and click OK. (Remember: eight characters. You can also use an extension with directory names, but few people do.) That's it. You've now got a new, empty directory, and you can put files in it. You can see it in the Tree window if it's expanded.

You can create subdirectories under your new directory by highlighting it and doing the same thing over again. For example, you might want to create subdirectories for different kinds of documents under the directory that holds your word processing program. Here you can see that the WP51 directory (it holds WordPerfect 5.1) has subdirectories and the DOCS subdirectory has subdirectories of its own.

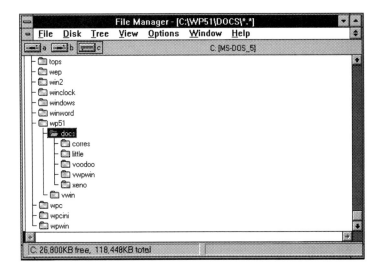

Sooner or later, you're going to want to remove a few files from your directories. But be careful: Make sure you really want to delete a file before you do it. Although DOS 5 has an UNDELETE command that can often rescue a file you've deleted by mistake, it can be tedious to get a deleted file back. And it can be impossible, if you've overwritten it with something else.

Deleting is the same as erasing. To delete, select the file or files you want to delete (Shift-click to select adjacent files, or Ctrl-click to select nonadjacent ones) and press the Del key or choose Delete from the File menu. You'll see a dialog box; double-check that the file name (or names) are the ones that you really want to delete; then click OK.

Deleting Files

▶ **Tip:** *Unlike deleting an icon in the Program Manager, deleting a file in the File Manager really removes it from your disk.*

If you want to delete files that are in other directories, you can type the path to them.

You can also use wildcards to delete a bunch of files at a time, such as OCTRPT?.WRI to delete all your OCTRPT1.WRI, OCTRPT2.WRI, OCTRPT3.WRI files, and so forth.

▶ **Tip:** *A quick way to erase disks is to do a Quick Format on them. Choose Format Disk from the Disk menu.*

But *be careful.* You can erase everything that's in a directory by entering *.* in the Delete: box. You may want to do this sometimes, especially to erase everything on a used floppy disk so that you can use it again— but be sure that it's really what you want to do.

Someday you'll probably want to delete a directory. The files in it may have become hopelessly outdated, for instance. The File Manager's File menu lets you delete a directory just like you delete a file.

DOS was very stubborn about letting people delete directories and absolutely refused to do it unless the directory was empty. The File Manager isn't so choosy, and it will let you delete a directory full of files if you turn off your confirmation prompts by using the Options menu, choosing Confirmation, and clicking to uncheck the Confirm on File Delete and Directory Delete prompts.

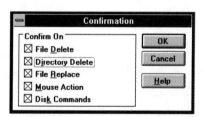

Because of this "feature," make sure you keep all your confirmations checked so that you don't delete a directory full of files by mistake!

Finding Files

You can spend a lot of time looking for a file. It gets worse if you're not even sure which file you're looking for. Windows has thankfully included a file-finding feature that can help you locate a file if you know its name, or even part of its name.

To search for a file, select Search from the File menu. In the dialog box that appears, type the name of the file you want to find.

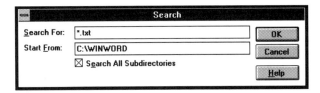

If you don't know the name of what you want to search for, try using wildcards. You may know that it begins with F, so you could enter F*.* to find everything beginning with F. If you know that it has a .TXT extension, enter *.TXT to find everything ending in .TXT. The dialog box will initially be set to *.*, which means everything, and you certainly don't want to search for *everything*, so enter *something* in the box!

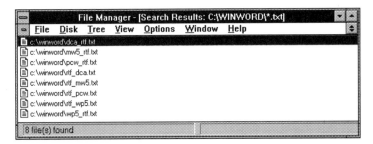

If you know the name of the file you're looking for but aren't quite sure how you spelled it, the ? wildcard can come in handy. Suppose you wanted to find a file named OLSON.WRI, but you weren't sure whether it was OLSON or OLSEN. Just enter *ols?n.wri,* or *ols?n.** if you're not sure of the extension.

Uncheck the Search All Subdirectories box if you don't want Windows to search your whole disk. If you have a large hard disk, this can take a while. With the box unchecked, Windows will search just the current directory and all its subdirectories. So if you want to search a specific directory, make it current before you use the Search command.

If you don't know anything about the file's name but do
know that you created it on a certain day, don't use the
Search command. Use the View menu instead and choose
Sort by Date. This is another way to locate files you're
looking for.

**Using the View
Menu**

You can use the File Manager's View menu and choose All
File Details to see the date and time each file was last saved
as well as the actual size of each file, in bytes.

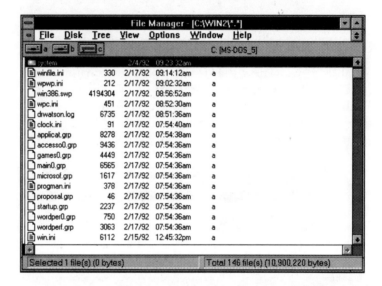

You probably don't need to see all this information all
the time. It's often useful to be able to see the last date you
changed a file, though. To see just this information,
choose Partial Details and then have Last Modification
Date.checked.

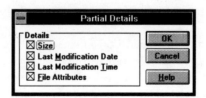

If you'd rather just see the documents that are associated with an application instead of all the files in a directory, such as font files and printer drivers, choose By File Type from the View menu and uncheck all but Documents. Here's where you can also choose to see just programs (.COM, .EXE,. .BAT, or .PIF files) or just directories.

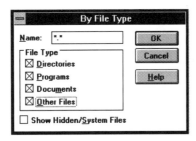

If all you want to see is document files with a certain extension—like .TXT files for the Notepad—change what's in the Name box to *.txt. The Name box usually has *.* in it. Remember, these wildcards mean "everything with any extension." You can substitute other patterns to restrict which file names will be displayed.

Sorting a Display

You can even tell Windows to sort your files so that you can see the most recent files first. To do this, choose Sort by Date from the View menu.

Another way of looking at files is alphabetically by file name. If you'd rather see them that way, choose Sort by Name from the View menu.

Starting Programs from the File Manager

As you saw in Chapter 3, you can also start programs by using the File Manager. This is a convenient way to start seldom-used programs that you don't want to put in a group. You saw how to use these two basic methods:

- Double-click on a program's icon.

- Use the Run command and enter the command used to start the program, including its path if necessary.

There are a couple more things you can do to start programs in the File Manager:

- Drag a document icon onto its program file icon (one of the tiny icons that look like a window) or onto a minimized program icon.

- Double-click on the icon of a document that's associated with a program.

- Select the file and press Enter, or choose Open from the File menu.

If you drag a document's icon onto its program's icon, that will start the program and open the document at the same time (you'll be asked to confirm that that's really what you want to do). If both aren't in the same directory, you'll need to arrange the directory windows so that you can see both the program's icon and the document's icon.

Getting these windows next to each other can be tricky, so use this tip on your Windows programs. Shift-click on the program file icon to start the program but make it run minimized. (If Shift-clicking won't start it, double-click on it to start it and then click its Minimize icon.) Now you're free to locate the document you want to open anywhere in your filing system. When you find it, drag its icon onto the minimized program icon at the bottom of your screen. The icon will change, showing that the file is in use. Just double-click on it to work with the document.

▶ Tip: *Shift-click on a program file icon to start it and minimize it at the same time.*

Associating Documents and Programs

If a document has been associated with a program, its icon has little lines on it. If you double-click on one of these icons, the program that's associated with the document will start and open the document. Most of the documents created in Windows programs are automatically associated with the program that created them, so you can start Windows Write just by clicking on one of its documents, for example. You can also associate non-Windows documents with their programs, so that you can start the program by clicking on an associated document.

To associate documents with programs, they must have an extension as part of their file name. It doesn't have to be three characters—even one character will do.

What you do when you associate documents with programs is tell Windows, "Look, all the files that end in .XXX (or .XX, or .X) belong to program AAA, so start that program whenever I double-click on one of those files, OK?"

To associate documents with a program, select one of the documents in a directory window, choose Associate from the File menu, and click on the program you want to associate the file with.

> **Tip:** *If your programs support OLE and your files are properly associated with the programs they belong to, you can use the File Manager to embed and link documents. Select the source document; then open the destination document. Drag the source document's icon to the destination to embed it; press Shift and Ctrl while you drag to link it.*

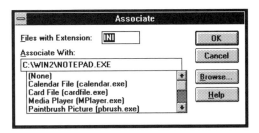

Click Browse if the program's name isn't listed. Once you click Browse, you can hunt through your directories to find the program.

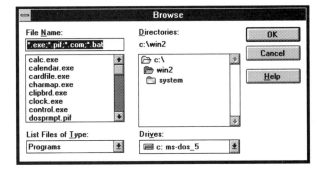

You only have to do this for one document; Windows automatically associates all the rest of the documents that have the same extension.

Adding Group Items with the File Manager

You can use the File Manager to add items to your Program Manager groups, too. Here's how to do it (you have to have a mouse).

Open the Program Manager and the File Manager and arrange them so that you can see the group window you want to add an item to. Then just drag the icon of the item you want to add from the File Manager window to the group window you want to add it to. Press Ctrl and drag it to make a copy instead of moving the item.

After you've added an item to a group, you can choose Properties from the Program Manager's File menu and change the icon's description, or even change the icon itself. You can add programs, documents, or just about anything else to your groups this way.

Copying Disks

What else can the File Manager do for you? Well, it also lets you copy floppy disks without going out to DOS. It's a little faster than using DOS, too. Here's how.

Put the disk you want to copy in your floppy disk drive and choose Copy Disk from the File menu. Then select the letter of the drive you're copying from (the source) and the drive you're copying to (the destination). If you only have one floppy drive, you won't get a dialog box where you can make these choices.

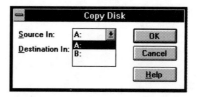

You'll be warned that any data on the destination disk will be erased. Click OK to start the copy process. Windows will copy what's on the disk (as much as it can), hold it in memory, and then copy it onto the destination disk. You'll be prompted to swap disks as necessary.

Your disks have to be the same capacity for you to use Windows' Copy Disk command. If they aren't the same capacity, you'll get a message saying, in effect, "Sorry." There's a way around this, though: Use the Copy command and copy *.* (everything) from one disk to another, as you saw earlier.

Another thing that the File Manager makes easy is formatting floppy disks. Instead of having to go out to DOS and do it, you can insert your blank floppy disk in drive A: (or B:) and choose Format Disk from the Disk menu.

Formatting Disks

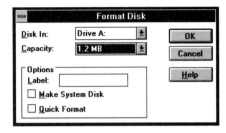

The capacity of your floppy disk drive will automatically appear in the Capacity box, so if you're formatting a double-density disk in a high-density disk drive, pick the lower capacity.

A caveat: High density isn't the same as double density. High-density disks hold a lot more than the regular kind, and they cost more, too. But if you format a double-density disk as a high-density disk, it won't work right. Look at the disk label before you format a disk.

How can you tell whether a disk needs to be formatted? If you aren't sure, put the disk in the floppy drive, close the drive door, and double-click on the File Manager's drive A: or B: icon. You'll get a message telling you that the disk needs to be formatted if it hasn't been formatted yet and asking if you want to format it.

If the disk is empty (formatted, but blank), you'll see a message at the bottom of the window telling you that the disk has so many bytes free. In that case, it doesn't have to be formatted; you can go ahead and use it for storing files. If there's anything on the disk, you'll see what it is and can decide whether you want to keep it or not. You can just delete what's on an already formatted disk instead of formatting it all over again. (See "Deleting Files" earlier in this chapter.)

Formatting a disk wipes out everything that's on it, but if you're running Windows under DOS 5, be aware that there's a neat UNFORMAT command you can use in most cases to recover data that was on a disk you formatted by mistake. If you remember before you use that disk for something else, that is.

Other File Manager Features

There are a lot of other things you can do with the File Manager, but we'll just mention a few of them here. You can explore them on your own after you've become more accustomed to Windows and to the File Manager's somewhat eccentric habits.

The Options menu lets you change a few things about how the File Manager's window appears. You can have everything displayed in lowercase, for example, or pick a different display font. If you'd like a larger, easier-to-read type style in your File Manager windows, choose a different or larger font.

The File Menu also lets you change a file's properties. For example, every file has a set of attributes that control whether it can be altered as well as whether it even shows up in a directory window. This is a fairly advanced topic, so we won't go into it, but here's one tip about how you can protect an important file.

To make sure that a file can't be deleted or changed, set its attributes to Read Only. Select the file; then choose Properties from the File menu and click the Read Only box.

```
┌────────────────────────────────────────────────┐
│ ▬      Properties for CHARMAP.HLP               │
│ File Name:    CHARMAP.HLP          ┌──────────┐ │
│ Size:         11,212 bytes         │   OK     │ │
│ Last Change:  12/17/91  03:10:00AM └──────────┘ │
│ Path:         C:\WIN2              ┌──────────┐ │
│                                    │  Cancel  │ │
│ ┌─Attributes────────────────┐     └──────────┘ │
│ │ ☐ Read Only   ☐ Hidden     │     ┌──────────┐ │
│ │ ☒ Archive     ☐ System     │     │   Help   │ │
│ └────────────────────────────┘     └──────────┘ │
└────────────────────────────────────────────────┘
```

Printing

You can even print from the File Manager. Select the document you want to print and choose Print from the File menu. Or (neat trick) drag a document's icon to the minimized Print Manager icon.

Here's a summary of the techniques you can use with the   **Quick Tips**
File Manager:

To	Do
Change the current drive	Click on a drive icon.
Open a directory folder	Double-click on a directory icon or press Enter when it's highlighted.
Expand a selected directory one level (if it's got a + on it)	Press +, click on it, or choose Expand One Level from the Tree menu.
Expand all the selected directory's subdirectories	Press * or choose Expand Branch from the Tree menu.
Expand all the subdirectories of all of the directories	Press Ctrl-* or choose Expand All from the Tree menu.
Collapse a branch	Press – or choose Collapse Branch.
Tile directory windows	Press Shift-F4 or choose Tile from the Window menu.
Cascade them	Press Shift-F5 or choose Cascade from Window menu.
Minimize a directory window	Click on its Minimize icon.
Select a file or directory	Click on it, or type the first letter of its name.
Select adjacent files and directories	Shift-click, or use Shift and the arrow keys.
Select nonadjacent files and directories	Ctrl-click.
Select the first file in the window	Press Home.
Select the last file in the window	Press End.
Select all files	Ctrl-/ or choose Select All from the File menu.
Deselect all files	Ctrl-\ or choose Deselect All from the File menu.
Deselect one file	Ctrl-click on it.

To	Do
Select groups of files	Shift-click to select the first group; then Ctrl-click to select the first file in the next group; then Shift-Ctrl-click on the last file in the group. Repeat Ctrl-click; Shift-Ctrl-click to add other groups to the selection.
Use wildcards	The * stands for any combination of characters, and ? stands for any one character.
Copy on the same disk	Select; then Ctrl-drag, or press F8 and use the Copy command.
Copy onto a different disk	Select; then drag, or press F8 and use the Copy command.
Move files and directories on the same disk	Select; then drag, or press F7 and use the Move command.
Move onto a different disk	Select; then Alt-drag, or press F7 and use the Move command.
Rename a file or directory	Select it; then choose Rename from the File menu.
Delete a file or directory	Select it; then choose Delete from the File menu.
Create a new directory	Click on the directory you want the new one to appear *under*, then choose Create Directory from the File menu.
Search for a file	Select Search from the File menu.
Search for a file by date	Select Sort by Date from the View menu.
Change the file information display	Use the View menu. Choose All File Detail sor Partial Details.
Start a program from the File Manager	Double-click on its icon, use the Run command, drag a document icon on top of its program file icon or a minimized program icon, or double-click on an associated document icon.
Associate documents	Select the document and choose Associate from the File menu; then choose the program you want to associate it with.

To	Do
Add an item to a Program Manager group from File Manager	Drag or Ctrl-drag the item's icon from the File Manager to the group.
Copy floppy disks	Choose Copy Disk from the Disk menu.
Format floppy disks	Choose Format Disk from the Disk menu.
Print files	Select the document and choose Print from the File menu, or drag a document's icon to the minimized Print Manager icon.

Customizing Windows

6

The Control Panel is where to go when you're ready to customize Windows. Here's where you change screen colors, make the mouse into a southpaw, set the date and time format, control how Windows acts with your network (if you're on one), and so forth.

Control Panel

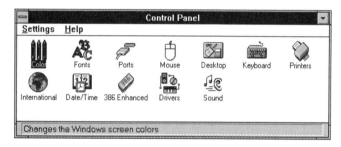

The Control Panel

To get to the Control Panel, click on the Program Manager and then double-click on the Main group icon. When you double-click on the Control Panel icon, you'll see icons for all its utilities:

- Color lets you change screen colors on the desktop and in windows. If you have a color monitor, of course.

- Fonts lets you add or remove fonts for your printer (more about this in the printing chapter).

- Ports lets you tell Windows which communication ports you're using.

- Mouse lets you change how fast the mouse pointer moves across the screen and set the double-click interval.

- Desktop is fun; it lets you change patterns used as your desktop's background. It also lets you change the cursor's blinking rate and set up a desktop grid.

- Keyboard lets you adjust the rate that keys repeat when you press and hold them down.

- Printers lets you add new printers and select the printer you want to use.

- International lets you use different number and currency formats, date and time formats, and so forth.

- Date/time lets you rest the system's date and time.

- 386 Enhanced lets you adjust how programs work with Windows in Enhanced mode. You won't see this one unless you have a 386 computer.

- Sound lets you assign sounds to events and turn the beep on and off. You need to have installed a sound card and speakers in your system to assign sounds to events or to have purchased a separate sound utility.

- Drivers lets you install and set up extra devices you've added to your system, such as video players and sound cards.

- Network lets you specify things about your network. You won't see this icon unless you're on a network that Windows recognizes.

Changing Screen Colors

If you don't have a color monitor, you can skip this part.

When you first start Windows, it comes with a color scheme already set up. It's more fun to choose one of the others, though, or create one of your own.

To choose one of the other color schemes, click on the Color icon. You'll see a sample window showing which window items can be changed to colors. (You'll only see the left-hand side until you choose Color Palette.)

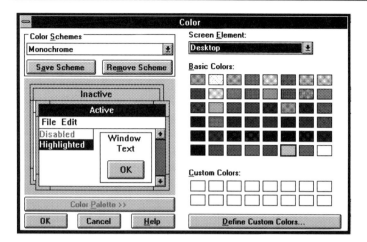

Press the down arrow key on the keyboard to cycle through the display of color schemes that have already been defined: Arizona (pale sand colors with blues and grays), Bordeaux (purples), Designer (gray-greens and a pattern), Fluorescent (need I say more?), monochrome (ugh), Ocean (soft blues and greens), Patchwork (reminiscent of a patchwork quilt, complete with dainty patterns), Rugby (maroon, blue, and yellow), Pastel (Easter egg colors), and Wingtips (browns and grays). Windows 3.1 adds practical specialized palettes for LCD and plasma displays, as well as fun ones like Hotdog Stand, Black Leather Jacket, and Valentine. Some of these you have to see to believe.

If you decide to use a different color scheme, click OK (or press Enter) when it's displayed.

Your Own Color Scheme

You can change these colors and even mix new shades of your own. First, choose one of the existing schemes that's closest to what you want. Then click on Color Palette. If you have a color monitor, you'll see an impressive array of colors and patterns. If you have a monochrome monitor, you'll see fewer colors, of course.

In the sample window on the left, click on the part you want to change, or press the down arrow when the Screen Element box is active to scroll through all the available choices. You can change the colors of the desktop, the application workspace, the window background, the window text, the menu bar and its text, the title bars (active and inactive) and title bar text, window borders (active and inactive), frames, the scroll bars, button colors, and highlight colors.

In the color palette part of the window, click on the color you want to use. You can choose from the basic colors or create custom colors of your own (more on this soon).

Here are a few personal tips for choosing colors. Keep the type that you'll be reading in a dark color, preferably black or dark blue. Keep the background—the application workspace—a very light tint, to keep it easy on your eyes for long stretches of time. Try a light green, light blue, or light yellow.

In fact, most of the other preassigned colors are probably too strong to use as a background color. If you want an easy-on-the-eyes light background, mix your own very pale shade (see below). Also keep the active title bar and the menu bar in a dark or strong color, so that you can read the words on them! If you want to use a light color there, use one with a pattern. The scroll bars and other places where you don't have to read? Go wild. Use magenta if you like, or any of the neon colors.

You can use a color scheme without saving it (just click OK or press Enter), but when you choose a different scheme, the selection of colors you chose will be lost. If you set up a combination of colors that you like, choose Save Scheme and type a name for the scheme. Give it a name that's different from the one it already has, so that you can tell which scheme's yours and which came with Windows.

If you create a lot of color schemes and later decide that some of them are really ugly, you can delete them with Remove Scheme.

Creating Custom Colors

You can "mix" 16 more custom colors and use them in your color schemes! Choose Define Custom Colors, and you'll see the Custom Color Selector dialog box. Wow! This book doesn't do it justice. The color box is an array of hues from orange to yellow to blue to purple to red, going from left to right.

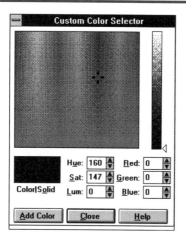

On this multicolored part of the screen, you'll see a small black "box"—four little black dots. That's the color refiner cursor. To change colors, drag that cursor until a color you like appears in the Color/Solid box. Once you've got the color you want, you can make it brighter or darker (adjust its luminosity) by dragging in the vertical luminosity bar. You can also adjust a color by clicking on the scroll arrows next to Hue (to change the color), Sat (to change the saturation, or purity of color), and Lum (to change the color's luminosity, or brightness).

As you change colors, you'll see the new color in the Color/Solid box. You can choose a solid color by clicking in the Solid part of the box. Click in the Color part of the box to choose the color pattern displayed there.

You can also change colors by typing in new values for them, or increase the amount of red, green, or blue in a color by clicking on the arrows next to the Red, Green, and Blue boxes.

Once you've created a custom color that you want to keep, select a box in the Custom Colors palette. (Windows will automatically fill these boxes from left to right if you don't select one, but you may want to group shades together.) Choose Add Colors to add the new color to the Custom Colors palette. You can then use your new color in any color scheme you like.

Changing Desktop Patterns

Desktop

Windows comes with a solid pattern for the desktop background. You can change it to a pattern (the pattern will be in the same color you chose for the desktop).

To choose a pattern, double-click on Desktop in the Control Panel. You'll see the Desktop dialog box (next page). In the Pattern portion, click on Edit Pattern and press the down arrow key on your keyboard (or click on the down scroll arrow on the screen) to see a list of patterns. Keep typing the down arrow to see samples of all the patterns. There are quite a few. If you see one you like, click OK. Click OK again to close the dialog box.

▶ **Tip:** *Keep Fast Alt+Tab Switching checked to quickly go between your application and the Program Manager.*

To create a custom pattern, first choose a pattern that's close to what you want. You'll see a sample of the pattern. This one's showing the Tulip pattern. It's nice, and so is the Waffle pattern (personal favorites.)

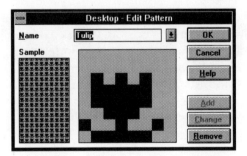

Click on the individual bits in the pattern to change it. This is one place you have to use a mouse!

On the left, you'll see a sample of the pattern as it'll look on the desktop. When you've got the pattern as you like it, click Change and then OK.

When you go back to the desktop, you'll see that pattern as the desktop background. You may need to minimize some windows to see the desktop.

The pattern you've created hasn't been saved yet. The next time you start Windows, it'll be gone. If you want to save a new pattern so that you can use it again, go back to the Edit Pattern dialog box and type a new name for it in the Name box; then click Add.

Hanging Wallpaper

Windows comes with a collection of graphic images called wallpaper that you can use for your desktop. You can choose one of these, or, if you have a scanner, you can use a graphic image that you've scanned.

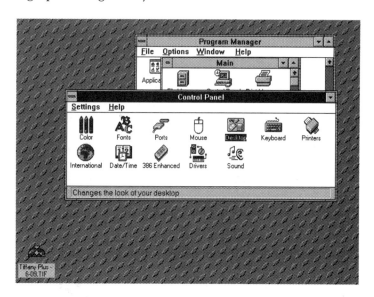

To choose one of Windows' wallpapers, click on the Control Panel's Desktop icon. Then click on the down scroll arrow next to the Wallpaper File box. Keep Tile checked to have the pattern repeat as many times as necessary to cover the whole desktop.

Click OK or press Enter to see the effects of your choice. Personal favorites: Flock, Redbrick, and Tartan, which are all very colorful. Steel is shown here because it's gray and reproduces better in this book.

> **Tip:** *Minimize icons to get them out of the way so that you can get the wallpaper's full effect.*

If you don't like any of the wallpapers, you can create your own. Windows Paintbrush saves images in bit-mapped (BMP) format, so you can use it to create your own wallpaper. You can also use Paintbrush to edit any of the wallpapers that are provided with Windows.

If memory's a consideration for you, don't use wallpaper. It's a memory hog.

You can't use a pattern for the desktop background and use wallpaper, too. If you've chosen both, Windows will use the wallpaper you've selected instead of the pattern as the desktop background. Set Wallpaper to None if you'd rather use a pattern.

If you've chosen a pattern and wallpaper, Windows will use the pattern as background for text used as icon labels. This can make them pretty hard to read, if not impossible. Set Pattern to None if you'd rather use wallpaper.

Screen Savers

Windows 3.1 comes with a set of screen savers that will automatically come on when you leave Windows unattended for a while. They theoretically protect your screen from burn-in, but in reality, they're just plain fun.

Once you choose a screen saver, click Test to see it in action. Click Setup to specify details about how you want it to look, such as choosing other colors and shapes, specifying the number of starts to show, and so forth. For Delay, set the number of minutes you want to elapse between the last time you used the keyboard or moved the mouse and the screen saver's coming on.

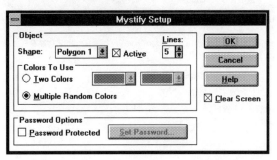

A handy Password box lets you assign a password to your screen saver so that nobody else can use Windows while you're away without first supplying the password. (Of course, they can turn your computer off and back on again, but that's cheating.) You can use up to 20 characters, including punctuation symbols, and capitalization doesn't count. If you forget your password, see the hint earlier in this paragraph (but you'll lose anything you haven't saved yet if you try that trick).

You can also adjust the windows' border width, control how icons appear on the desktop, and set how fast you want the cursor to blink. Like the pattern and wallpaper options, you won't see the effects of your changes until you click OK. If you just click outside the box, no changes take place; you just make a different window active.

Other Desktop Options

If your icons are so close together that their names overlap, you can change the space between them by clicking on the arrows next to Icon Spacing. The preset value is 75 pixels (a pixel is one screen dot), but you can change it up to 512 for v-e-r-y wide spacing between icons. I keep mine around 125 so that "Non-Windows Applications," which is probably typical of the longest group name you'll have, won't overlap with anything.

To see the effects of changing icon spacing, click OK, go to the Program Manager, and then choose Arrange Icons from the Program Manager's Window menu. (Arrange Icons only arranges the icons in the active window.)

If you're neat and orderly and you want windows to align nicely and icons to always align on an invisible grid on the desktop, choose the Granularity box and enter the number of pixels you want between grid lines (1 to 49), or click on the arrows to change 8 pixels at a time. To turn off the grid, enter 0. Windows comes with the grid off. I kept mine off at first but later found I liked it better with it on.

To change the width of the borders, click on the arrows next to Border Width in the Desktop dialog box. The smallest border you can have is 1 and the widest is 49. I keep mine at 3, the default, because I like thin borders. That's what you see in the figures in this book.

You'll have to experiment with all these settings until you get them the way you like them, because you don't see the effects until you click OK to close the dialog box.

One last option in the Desktop dialog box lets you change the rate of the cursor's blink. Slide the scroll box in the Cursor Blink Rate box to Fast or Slow and see how fast it blinks. Click OK when the rate's as you want it.

Customizing the Keyboard

To change the rate a key repeats when you hold it down, double-click on the Keyboard icon in the Control Panel. You'll see the Keyboard dialog box.

Keyboard

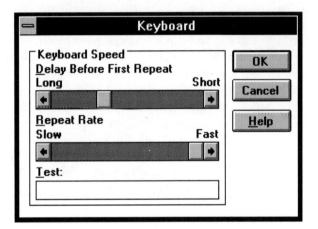

Move the box in the Key Repeat Rate to adjust the rate. Try it out by typing any key and holding it down in the Test Typematic box. Click OK to save your setting.

Customizing the Mouse

You can set the mouse's tracking and double-click speed and change it from a right-handed mouse to a left-handed one.

Mouse

When you open the Mouse icon, you'll see the Mouse dialog box. To change the tracking speed (the rate the mouse zips across your screen as you move it on the real desktop), drag the box in the Tracking Speed scroll bar. When you get accustomed to using the mouse, you may want to turn up the speed.

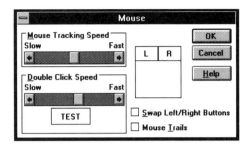

Windows interprets two "quick" clicks as a double-click. As you know, a double-click often produces a very different result from a single click. If your double-clicks are being interpreted as two single clicks, change the double-click response rate. You can test it out by double-clicking in the TEST box. It will change from white to black (or vice versa) when you're double-clicking fast enough for the setting you've chosen.

If you're left-handed, reverse the actions of the left and right mouse buttons by selecting the Swap Left Right Buttons box. Again, you can test out the new settings in the L/R box.

Remember, if you switch them, you have to switch them back by clicking with the right mouse button, not the left!

Mouse Trails is for those of you who have a laptop with an LCD display, which is sometimes hard to read. Checking this box has the mouse leave a "trail" of pointers to improve visibility.

Instead of setting the date and time with the DOS DATE and TIME commands, you can double-click on the Date/Time icon. Just type in a new date or time, or click on the arrows to adjust the date and time shown.

Setting the Date and Time

Date/Time

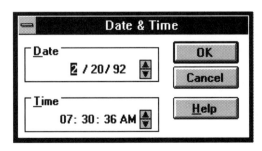

Other Options

International

Use the International option to change the format of the date and time.

Use the International icon to set different formats for the date and time, currency, measurements (English or metric), and number formats. When you double-click on this icon, you'll see the International dialog box. If you're using Windows in English, you probably won't need to change the settings, except maybe for date and time, if you want military-style dates and times, like 15 March 1991 and 23:55.

```
┌─────────────────────────────────────────────────┐
│ ─              International                      │
│ Country:       United States        ▼   ┌──OK──┐ │
│ Language:      English (American)   ▼   │Cancel│ │
│ Keyboard Layout: US                 ▼   │ Help │ │
│ Measurement:   English              ▼            │
│ List Separator:  ,                               │
│ ┌Date Format──────────┐ ┌Currency Format───────┐ │
│ │ 2/20/92   [Change..] │ │ $1.22    [Change..]  │ │
│ │ Thursday, February 20, 1992 │ ($1.22)         │ │
│ ┌Time Format──────────┐ ┌Number Format─────────┐ │
│ │ 07:33:54 AM [Change..]│ │1,234.22  [Change..] │ │
└─────────────────────────────────────────────────┘
```

If you're running a network, you'll see a Network icon in the Control Panel. Use it to change your user ID, switch to a different password, and so forth. The dialog box you see will depend on the network you're connected to.

Ports

Use the Ports icon to specify the settings for the communications ports (COM1, COM2, and so forth) your computer uses. If you buy a modem or a serial printer (like some laser printers) or attach a serial mouse to one of these ports, you may need to change the settings. Whatever hardware you bought should have a manual with it that tells you what settings to use.

386 Enhanced

If your computer is a 386, you'll see an icon for 386 Enhanced mode. If you're an advanced user, you can use it to fine-tune how Windows uses memory and interacts with non-Windows applications and devices like printers and modems.

Windows 3.1 lets you add sounds—and more—to your system. To play sounds, you must have installed a sound card and speakers in your computer. Once that's installed, you can click on the Sound icon and assign a sound to a specific "event," such as when Windows is requesting more information or sounding a warning.

The Drivers Control Panel is necessary for installing drivers—software that controls, or "drives" various devices that you add, such as videodisc players and CD-ROM drives to take advantage of Windows 3.1's multimedia capabilities. Once you've installed the drivers via this Drivers Control Panel, you can use the Media Player accessory to play animation and sound files.

Using Sound

Sound

Drivers

Media Player

Customizing Help

In addition to customizing Windows with the Control Panel, you can also customize Windows Help. If you find that there are Help topics you refer to over and over, you can mark them with a bookmark so that you can locate them quickly. Choose Bookmark and then Define from the Help menu when the topic you want to create the bookmark for is displayed. Then enter a short name for your bookmark and click OK. After you've created a bookmark, you can quickly locate that topic by choosing Bookmark and then clicking on the name you gave it. Windows will take you straight to that topic.

You can also annotate Help topics with personal notes about your own problem areas and things you forget all the time. To do this, choose Edit and then Annotate from the Help menu. You'll see a notepad where you can write your notes. After you've annotated a topic, you'll see a paper clip next to its name.

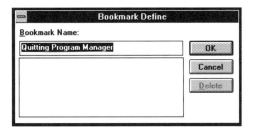

You can even copy annotations and paste them into other annotations or paste text from documents into annotations.

Here's a tip: Instead of annotating a help window or making a bookmark for it, if you want to keep it handy during a session with Windows, just find the topic you need and then minimize the window.

Quick Tips

Here's a rundown of the techniques you saw in this chapter.

To	Do
Change the screen colors	Click on the Control Panel's Color icon; then choose a color scheme or create your own.
Change the desktop pattern	Click on the Desktop icon; then choose Edit Pattern.
Choose a desktop wallpaper	Click on the Desktop icon; then choose a wallpaper.
Choose a screen saver	Click on the Desktop icon; then choose a screen saver.
Change the windows' border width, icon spacing, grid, and/or cursor blink rate	Click on the Desktop icon and choose any of these.
Change the rate keys repeat	Click on the Keyboard icon and change the key repeat rate.
Change the way the mouse operates	Click on the Mouse icon and set the tracking speed, left/right-handed mouse, etc.
Change the system date and time	Click on the Date and Time icon.
Change the date and time format	Click on the International icon.
Create a Help bookmark	Go to the topic and choose Bookmark from the Help menu.
Annotate a Help topic with your own notes	Go to the topic and choose Annotate; then type the notes.

Printing

You probably installed a printer when you installed Windows, or maybe someone else set it up for you. If you've been printing just fine with no problems, you may not even be interested in this chapter. But if you haven't installed a printer, if you've bought new fonts for your printer, or if you're having trouble printing, you may find some valuable information here.

Windows uses a special utility called the Print Manager to do printing. It automatically takes over when you print and sends your print jobs to your printer so that you can keep right on working. If you send a big document to be printed, though, you may have to wait just a bit for it to get to the Print Manager.

You'll see the Print Manager icon at the bottom of the screen while it's printing your documents, if the desktop's not covered with windows.

To check on what the Print Manager is up to, click on its icon. (It's in the Main group if the Print Manager isn't printing.) You can also press Ctrl+Esc to bring up the Task List and then select Print Manager. You'll see the Print Manager window. It shows you the status of all your print jobs and lets you change the order they'll be printed in, among other things.

The Print Manager

Print Manager

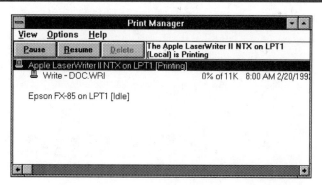

Changing the Print Queue

As you send each print job, Print Manager places it in a queue, or lineup, and prints each one in the order it gets them, like a short-order cook. You can look at how the documents are lined up in this print queue and change the order they'll be printed in, if you're in a rush for a particular document.

To change the printing order, just drag the icon of the document to a new location in the print queue. You can't change the order of the one that's printing, though (it has a little printer icon to the left of it).

As you print, you may need to stop the printer temporarily ("pause" it) to stop a paper jam or whatever. To do this, click on the Pause button. When you've fixed the problem, click the Resume button.

Stop That Job!

If you want to cancel printing of a document that's being printed *right now,* click the Delete button. You'll be asked to confirm that you really want to stop printing, so click Cancel in the dialog box. The printer may not stop right away because it will continue to print whatever part of the document has already been sent to it. If you can't live with that, there's always a power switch on your printer.

If you decide that you'd rather not print a document that's waiting in the queue, select it by clicking on it; then click Delete.

▶ **Tip:** *Stopping printing everything.*

If you want to cancel printing *everything,* here's the quick way: just exit the Print Manager (choose Exit from the Options menu or double-click on the Control icon). You'll be asked if that's really what you want to do.

To close the Print Manager window without canceling all your printing, minimize it by clicking on the Minimize icon in the upper-right corner.

You can use the Print Manager's Options menu to speed up the printing process. Normally Windows divides the time it pays attention to your programs and to printing about equally. You can choose High Priority to allocate more attention to printing (and thus speed it up and perhaps slow down your work in a program) or Low Priority if the work you're doing is more important than how fast your documents get printed.

Print Manager Options

The Print Manager sometimes needs to get your attention to deal with printing problems. Your printer may have run out of paper, or paper may have jammed inside it, for example. Normally it will beep once at you and then flash the Print Manager's icon (or the Print Manager's title bar, if you've got it open as a window). You can change the way the Print Manager gets your attention to either have it beep and show you a message box whenever it needs your care, no matter what program you're running, or have the Print Manager ignore the condition and just stop printing whenever it has to. Use the Options menu to change how you want this to work.

Getting Messages

If you're sharing printers with other users on a network, printing is just a little different. If you're using the Print Manager over a network, you'll need to choose Network Settings and connect to the net via the Options menu.

In some cases it may be faster to print to the network directly. If this is true on your particular network, choose Network Settings and check the Print Net Jobs Direct box.

When you do network printing, you don't see the Print Manager's icon, so don't even bother looking for it. If you need to see the Print Manager's window, select the Print Manager from the Main group.

Network Printing

Printing from Non-Windows Programs

If you're printing a document from a non-Windows program, you don't use the Print Manager at all. You just print as you normally would from that program. (Sometimes—a very few sometimes—your document won't print until you exit from Windows.)

You may run into trouble if you try to print some documents from a non-Windows program and then go over to Windows and print with the Print Manager. Windows may get confused with all this happening at the same time. Print non-Windows documents and then print from Windows, or vice versa. It doesn't matter which you do first; just don't do both together and you shouldn't have any problems.

As a last resort, if you're having trouble printing a non-Windows document, you can probably convert it into a format that a Windows program can use. For example, most word processing programs let you convert their documents to ASCII format (sometimes called DOS Text format) or to some "generic word processor" format. The Notepad and Windows Write can accept and print these files. Microsoft Excel, if you have it, can read dBASE and Lotus 1-2-3 files, as well as other spreadsheet formats.

Adding Printers

Printers

You probably installed a printer when you installed Windows, or someone else did. But if you buy a new printer, you may need to know how to install it. This section will tell you how in general, but there's a lot of online help available as you install a particular printer. As you're installing, as soon as you select your printer, choose Help to get specific help about that model of printer.

To install a new printer, first find the Windows Setup disks. You're going to need one of them. Then double-click the Control Panel's Printers icon. You'll see the Printers dialog box, and it should list any printers that have already been installed.

You can install more than one printer, and they don't all have to be connected to your computer. If you have one kind of printer at home and another one at work, you can install both of them so that you can format documents for your work printer even if you're working at home. On second thought, maybe you'd rather not do this, so you'll have an excuse for not working at home.

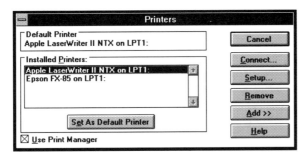

Click on Add; then select your printer from the list that appears. To go quickly to the name of your printer, type the first letter of its name (very handy if yours is a Wang). You can then use the down arrow to move to the each printer name you want. When your printer is highlighted, click Install. You'll be asked to insert a Windows Setup disk (the screen will tell you which one) so that Windows can copy the information it needs.

If your printer isn't listed, there are two easy things you can do. First, you can get out your printer manual and see if it will emulate another printer that is on the list. Second, you can choose Generic/Text Only. With it, you can print your documents with text but no graphics, at least until you get a call in to Microsoft about what to do about installing your printer. The phone number for Windows technical support is (206) 637-7098. They're constantly adding support for more printers.

You can also choose Unlisted Printer, but you'll need to know where your printer driver files are (and *what* they are), because you'll be asked to tell Windows that.

Setting up Your Printer

After you choose which printer you want to install, click Setup. You'll see a Setup box specifically for the printer you're installing. What you can choose depends on the printer (this box is for a HP DeskJet 500).

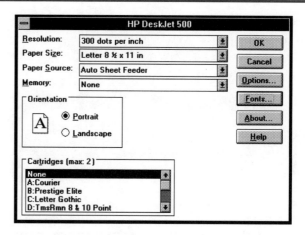

Click Options to specify other things you can choose about this printer, such as the print quality and the darkness of printed graphics. Click Fonts to install any additional fonts you've bought for your printer.

The Default Printer   After you've got everything as you want it, click OK. You'll return to the Printers dialog box, where you can choose which printer you want to be the default printer—the one you want to print with. Windows prints with the default printer, even though you may have several printers installed.

Look in the Default Printer box to see which printer Windows is going to use as your default printer. If the printer listed there isn't the one you want to print with, double-click on the name of the printer you *do* want to print with. All of your installed printers are listed right there on the screen.

Fonts   If you're brand-new to Windows, you may be surprised to find out that you can now change fonts on the screen! Windows comes with several different fonts that are automatically installed in your system, depending on what kind of printer you have and what kind of display monitor you're using. If you don't believe me, go into Windows Write and use the Character menu to change fonts.

Windows 3.1 comes with new TrueType fonts that are automatically installed when you install Windows. What's neat about these TrueType fonts is that they look on the screen just as they'll look in your printed documents. And because they take up a lot less room on your hard disk, you can store lots more fonts.

TrueType fonts are different from the fonts you may have been using because a mathematical language is used to create them. As a result, you can have fonts in all sorts of weird sizes, like 11.5 points. And because you don't have to have an expensive PostScript printer to print TrueType fonts, you can get the sophisticated effects of PostScript on LaserJets and some dot-matrix printers, too.

But let's back up and review font basics.

A font is basically a collection of characters in a particular typeface. All printers, even laser printers, have at least one font built into them, and it's usually Courier, which looks like this:

Font Basics

```
Courier
```

Yes, it's supposed to look like a typewriter, but why anyone would want to have an expensive laser printer produce "typewriter" type is beyond me. Courier is a monospaced font, which means that each letter takes up the same amount of space as any other letter. With a proportionally spaced font, like the ones used on this book, each letter takes up a different amount or space; for example, an *i* takes up less space than an *m*. Looks better, yes?

There are basically two different types of fonts : serif fonts, which have little things at the ends of the letters, like the text of this book, and sans serif fonts, which have very clean lines and are like the text used for the headings in this book. Purists say that serif fonts are easier to read if you're reading a lot at one stretch. I agree with them.

The fonts you see on your screen are called screen fonts, which you'll also see called bitmapped fonts. They *represent* what you get in your documents. Your display monitor often can't display everything just exactly as it will be printed, although line breaks and so on are displayed correctly.

The fonts used to print documents are called printer fonts. You'll probably have a wider variety of printer fonts to choose from than screen fonts, but Windows will represent the font that's chosen as closely as it can on the screen.

Then TrueType came along. With TrueType fonts, screen fonts and printer fonts are the same thing, which simplifies things immensely. You can tell TrueType fonts from the others because they'll either have (TrueType) or (TT) listed next to them in your programs' dialog boxes,and they won't show a point size next to them because they're available in all point sizes.

There are also plotter fonts, which are also called stroke fonts. These will look the same on any printer, but they're not very pretty, and they're very slow to print. An old joke has it that they're called stroke fonts because a typesetter had one when he saw them.

Fonts are also described in terms of size. A font's size is measured in points (1/72 of an inch). Commonly used sizes in printed documents are 10- or 12-point type for text (roughly corresponding to Pica or Elite on a type-writer) and larger point sizes, such as 14 points, for headings. Dot-matrix printers also use the notation cpi (characters per inch) for font sizes.

Adding Fonts To add new screen fonts, double-click on the Fonts icon. You'll see the Fonts dialog box. As you click on each font, a sample of what the characters in the font look like is shown

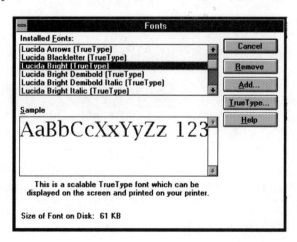

at the bottom of the box. If you see several different sizes
listed for a font, that means that it's available only in those
sizes. If no size is shown, it's a TrueType font or a plotter font,
and the screen will tell you which.

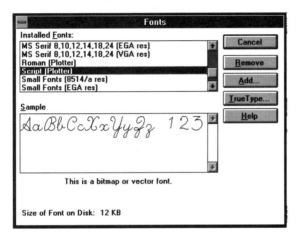

To add new screen or TrueType fonts that you purchase
to the list, click on Add. Windows will search its system directory for all files ending in .FON. Click other directory folders
to locate the directory where your fonts are stored. If you're
installing fonts from floppy drive A or B, click on its icon.

To install printer fonts, click on the Printers icon in the
Control Panel. Then click on the printer you want to install
the fonts for, in the list of installed printers, and click on Setup.
Click Fonts. (If there's no Fonts button, you can't add new fonts
to that particular printer.) Click on it to go to the Font Installer.

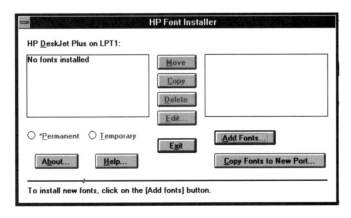

You can then click on Add Fonts... or the ever-useful Help button. If you click Add, Windows will ask you to insert the disk with the font files on it in drive A:. If you've already copied the font files onto your hard disk, fill out the dialog box with the name of the drive and directory where the files are. Windows will then search the floppy disk or the directory on your hard disk and display a list of all the font files it finds. Click Help if you need help installing them; the procedure is slightly different for different kinds of printers.

Your printer may have printer fonts that Windows doesn't have screen fonts for. That's OK. Windows will substitute a font on the screen that's about the same as the printer font. It just won't look exactly as it will when it's printed.

Saving Disk Space

Fonts use up a lot of memory. If there's one you never use, you can free up some disk space by deleting it. There's a Remove box for screen fonts and a Delete box for printer fonts, depending on which dialog box you're looking at.

If you want to make the most of your disk space, use TrueType fonts only. Since you don't have to store separate bitmapped versions of each point size you want to use, they take up a lot less space than regular fonts. If you want to stick to TrueType exclusively, click the TrueType button in the Fonts dialog box and make sure that they're enabled and that you've checked that you want to use them in all your applications. You can then delete other fonts that are cluttering up your disk, but don't delete the MS Sans Serif font (called Helv in Windows 3.0), because it's the one that's used in dialog boxes. (You can probably get rid of those plotter fonts, though.)

Font Managers

You can also purchase font management programs that will help you manage your fonts. ATM (Adobe Type Manager) is one of these, but there are lots of others (Bitstream's FaceLift, MicroLogic's MoreFonts, LaserTools' Fonts-on-the-Fly, etc.) What these programs do is create screen fonts for you as they're required, so that you don't have to store separate bitmapped fonts for each point size you want to see on the screen. These font managers also scale and generate the fonts and print them on any printer that Windows supports, so here again you get the benefits of PostScript without having to buy an expensive PostScript printer. If you aren't using TrueType fonts exclusively, get yourself a font management program.

Sometimes things don't always work as you'd like them to, and printing is one area where this seems to happen more frequently than most of us would like. If the printer won't print, here are a few things to check for, more or less in order of difficulty.

Troubleshooting Printing Problems

Check to see that it's on. Check that it has paper. See if the cables are tightly connected.

In Windows, go to the Print Manager and check the printer queue. Try deleting all the print jobs except the top one. If that doesn't do it, check to see that the printer you've intended to print the document on is the default printer.

If you can only print one document at a time, the best bet is that the Print Manager has gotten turned off. Likewise, if you can't continue working on something else while your document is printing, the Print Manager's off. Go to the Printers icon in the Control Panel and check that Use Print Manager box.

Try printing from Notepad or Write. If you can print from there, the problem is probably in your application program, not in Windows.

Try printing with the Print Manager off and see if that will solve the problem.

If you've tried all these things and it still won't print, exit Windows and try printing from another program. If it prints from there, you know the problem is somewhere in Windows. Go back into Windows and double-check your setup, including the Printer Setup dialog box in whatever program you're trying to print from (it'll be on the Print menu). If all else fails, install your printer again. If it still won't work, call Microsoft (206/637-7098). Before you call, make sure that you know the printer's make and model, what program (and its version) you're using, and what you've done so far to try to solve the problem.

Sometimes the printer will print, but you won't like what you see. Check out the PRINTERS.WRI file that comes with Windows (it's a Write document) and see if it has any hints about your specific printer.

Sometimes the problem is that you're not getting the fonts you asked for. If this happens, it's probably one of two things: either the fonts aren't there (you forgot to download them, or you may have turned the printer off, or there may have been a power failure, or you may not have shoved your font cartridge all the way into its slot) or your printer's out of memory. Fonts are memory hogs, and if you're printing graphics, too, you can easily run out of printer memory. To get around this, print the document using the printer's built-in fonts or use fewer fonts in the document. Split the document into smaller files, if it's lots of graphics that's causing the problem.

If the problem is that the fonts on the screen don't match the fonts you see in your document, you're probably not using TrueType and not using a font management program. What's happening is that Windows is using a font that looks like the printer font your document is calling for, but it isn't quite the same. To make sure that what you see is what you get, use TrueType, get a font management package, or make sure that each font you install has matching screen fonts for each of its printer fonts.

Here's a rundown of the techniques you saw in this **Quick Tips** chapter:

To	Do
Print a non-Windows document	Use the print command in the program.
Check on the Print Manager	Click on its icon, or press Ctrl+Esc and choose it from the Task List
Change a document's position in the print queue	Drag the document's icon or use Ctrl-Up or -Down arrow in the Print Manager screen.
Pause the printer	Click Pause or press Alt+P.
Resume printing	Click Resume or press Alt+R.
Stop printing a job or remove a job from the queue	Click Delete or press Alt+D.
Cancel printing everything	Double-click on the Print Manager's Control icon or choose Exit from the Options menu.
Close the Program Manager without cancelling printing	Click on its Minimize icon.
Add a new printer	Click on the Control Panel's Printers icon.
Add new screen fonts	Click on the Control Panel's Fonts icon.
Add new printer fonts	Click on the Control Panel's Printers icon.

Oh, No! (Trouble-shooting)

Setup Problems

Help! My system locked up during setup. You're going to need to restart your computer. But before you try running Setup again, check your AUTOEXEC.BAT file and see if there are any commands in it that start memory-resident programs running. To read it, give this command at the DOS prompt: *type autoexec.bat | more.* If there are any, read the file SETUP.TXT that comes with Windows. It's on Disk 1. To read it, assuming it's in drive A, give this command at the DOS prompt: *type a:setup.txt | more.* To see each page, press Enter. To get out of it, press Ctrl+C.

The SETUP.TXT file may give you instructions about changing your AUTOEXEC.BAT file. If you have to do that, first make a copy of your AUTOEXEC.BAT file just in case you edit something vital. At the command line, give this command: *copy autoexec.bat autoexec.xxx.* That way, you can always get your original file back by renaming AUTOEXEC.XXX AUTOEXEC.BAT.

Now, as for editing it. You can edit it in your word processing program. Remember to save it in ASCII format or DOS Text format, whatever your program calls it. If you're running DOS 5, you can edit it in the Editor by giving this command at the command line: *edit autoexec.bat.* The DOS 5 Editor automatically saves files in ASCII format, so you don't have to worry about any special format.

Now try running Setup again. If it still doesn't work right, try starting Setup with this command *setup /i.* This will allow you to do a custom setup and tell Windows exactly what system components you have (better figure it out first; get out all those manuals). Sometimes Windows doesn't correctly determine what hardware you have.

Mouse Problems

My mouse won't work! There are two kinds of mice, bus mice and serial mice. A serial mouse usually has a round connector and a bus mouse has a big plug-type connector. If you have a serial mouse, make sure it's attached to the COM1 or COM2 port on the back of your computer. If it's on COM3 or COM4, it won't work with Windows. Get out your manual or call a friend if you can't figure out which port's which. I never can.

The mouse pointer jumps all over the screen! The simplest explanation of all is that your mouse needs cleaning. They pick up all sorts of dirt and lint in their moving parts, or balls.

You can use the Mouse Control Panel to change the mouse's tracking speed (see Chapter 6 for details), and that may clear up the problem. If that doesn't do it, the problem's probably being caused by something called an "interrupt conflict," and you'll need to get out your mouse manual and figure it out.

Problems as You Work

I'm out of memory! How can you tell? Your system runs slowly. Your hard disk in-use light keeps blinking, indicating that Windows is furiously swapping data around to make the best use of what little memory you have. If this is happening, close a few programs. Minimize as many icons as you can. Don't use wallpaper. Empty the Clipboard. Get out of all non-Windows programs. That should do it.

It's running so s-l-o-w... If this only happens from time to time, you're probably low on memory. Close a few programs. There are other, more major things you can do to optimize memory, but this is the easiest. The others involve changing various software settings, working with your hardware, or both. If it runs slow all the time, you probably need one of these harder solutions.

Help! I can't get out of my program! If you're in a non-Windows program, you'll need to do whatever is normal in that program to exit from it. Double-clicking on the Control icon in a non-Windows program won't let you exit from the program.

If exiting in the normal way doesn't do it, try pressing Esc. Then press Alt+Tab and see if you don't get back to Windows. If not, try pressing Ctrl+Alt+Del. In Windows 3.1, this will quit your application without shutting down your system. When you press Ctrl+Alt+Del, you'll see a message about what you can do.

It just beeps at me! Check the title bar. If it says "Select" or "Mark," press the right mouse button, or press Esc. If it says "Scroll," press one of the arrow keys, or press Esc. What's happening is that Windows thinks you want to select something to put on the Clipboard or scroll through the document.

If it doesn't say "Select" or "Mark" or "Scroll" on the title bar, press Alt+Enter. If that doesn't work, press Ctrl+Alt+Del to quit the program you're running without shutting down your system.

When I press a key, something else happens! If you press a key combination that you expect will do one thing and it does another, you're probably using a shortcut key. Go out to the Program Manager, highlight the icon of the program you were running, and choose Properties from the File menu. Check to see if any shortcut keys have been assigned to the program. If not, and it's happening in a non-Windows program, check the program's program information file (PIF). Double-click on the PIF Editor's icon in the Main group; then choose Open. You'll see a list of all the PIFs that Windows has created. Pick the one for the program that's causing the trouble; then click the Advanced button you'll see in the dialog box that appears. At the bottom of the box, you'll see any shortcuts that are reserved for that program.

I tiled all the windows, but I still can't see everything!
The Program Manager's probably in the way. Minimize it.

Problems with Non-Windows Programs

I Can't paste into my non-Windows program! You're probably trying to paste graphics, and you won't be able to. There's nothing wrong with you or your program. It just won't work. You can only paste text into most non-Windows programs.

If you're not trying to paste graphics, try this. Open the program's PIF (see above) and see is Allow Fast Paste is checked. If it is, uncheck it.

How the *&*% do I select things to copy to the Clipboard in a non-Windows program? If you've got a mouse and can run the program in a window, you shouldn't have any problem. Just select with the mouse and use the Control menu's Edit menu to copy. The Windows mouse will take over whenever a program's in a window, so your program doesn't even have to support a mouse.

If you've got a mouse but can only run the program full-screen, you shouldn't have any problem, either, as long as the program you're using can use a mouse. You just use the mouse to select things.

If the program will run in a window and you *don't* have a mouse, it's even more complicated. Press Al+Space bar to open the window's Control menu; then choose Edit and Mark. You can then use the keyboard to select text to be copied to the Clipboard. Put the cursor at the start of what you want to copy, press the Shift key, and then press the arrow keys until what you want to copy is highlighted. Press Alt+Space bar again and choose Copy.

If your program can't run in a window and you don't have a mouse, you're out of luck.

When I copy spreadsheet data, it's all jumbled up! You're probably using a nonproportional font. With this kind of font, each letter or number takes up a different amount of space. Use a nonproportional font like Courier, or put tabs between the columns.

I can't run my non-Windows programs! During Setup, Windows looks for non-Windows programs and creates program information files (PIFs) for them. If you start a non-Windows program that there's no PIF for (one that you've added after setting up Windows, for example), Windows uses a default PIF. If your program isn't running, you can try editing its PIF or modifying the default PIF (use the PIF Editor and enter *_default.com* as the Program Filename). These topics are pretty advanced, so better click away on the Help button or get out one of those bigger books or the Windows manual.

What was that phone number again? Microsoft Product Support is (206) 637-7098. But before you call, read all the text files that came with Windows to see if there's a hint in them about your problem. If you're still stuck, make sure that you have a pretty good idea of what your system is— what kind of hardware you have, the directory where Windows is installed, what kind of mouse you're using, and so forth. Make notes on what you were doing when the problem occurred, and what you've tried so far to fix it. It will also be helpful to print out a copy of your AUTOEXEC.BAT and CONFIG.SYS files or have them handy on the screen, because whoever answers the phone at Microsoft will probably ask you what's in them.

Getting More Help

Here's How

To	Do
Add a document to a program item	Add the document's name to the end of the line in the Program Item Properties dialog box. (Choose New from the Program Manager's File menu; then choose New Program Item.)
Add a program to a group via Setup	Double-click on the Setup icon (Main group); choose Options and then Set Up Applications.
Add an item to a Program Manager group from the File Manager	Open both a File Manager window and a group window. Drag the program's icon from the File Manager to the group.
Add an item to a group	Copy or move the program's icon into the group (press Ctrl and drag to copy it; drag to move it). Or choose New from the Program Manager's File menu; click Program Item; fill out a description and a command line.
Add a new printer	Click on the Control Panel's Printer icon.
Add new fonts	Click on the Control Panel's Fonts icon.
Annotate a Help topic with your own notes	Go to the topic and choose Annotate; then type the notes.
Associate documents with a program	Select the document and choose Associate from the File Manager's File menu; then choose the program you want to associate it with.

To	Do
Cancel a print job	Highlight the job and click Delete in the Print Manager window, or press Alt+D.
Cancel printing everything	Double-click on the Print Manager's Control icon or choose Exit from the Options menu.
Cascade windows	Choose Cascade from the Windows menu, or press Shift+F5.
Change the file information display	Use the View menu and choose All File Detaissl or Partial Details.
Change how File Manager windows appear	Use the Options menu.
Change an item's icon	Click Change Icon in the Program Item Properties dialog box.
Change the system date and time	Click on the Control Panel's Date and Time icon.
Change print speed, message method, or print on a network	Use the Print Manager's Options menu.
Change a group's name	Click its icon; choose File and then Properties.
Change the current drive	Click on a drive icon .
Change the rate keys repeat	Click on the Keyboard icon and change the key repeat rate (Control Panel).
Change the screen colors	Click on the Control Panel's Color icon; then choose a color scheme or create your own.
Change the way the mouse operates	Click on the Mouse icon and set the tracking speed, left/right handed mouse, etc.
Change a document's position in the print queue	Drag the document's icon or use Ctrl-Up or -Down arrow in the Print Manager screen.
Change the windows' border width, icon spacing, grid, and/or cursor blink rate	Click on the Control Panel's Desktop icon and choose any of these.

To	Do
Change the desktop pattern	Click on the Control Panel's Desktop icon; then choose Edit Pattern.
Choose a desktop wallpaper	Click on the Control Panel's Desktop icon; then choose a wallpaper.
Choose an item in a dialog box	Click on the selection, or type Alt+*letter* (where *letter* is the letter in the box).
Choose a screen saver	Click on the Desktop icon; then choose a screen saver.
Close the File Manager	Choose Exit from the File menu, or double-click on the File Manager's Control icon, or choose End Task for the File Manager from the Task List.
Close a window	Double-click on its Control icon (or press Ctrl+F4 or Alt+F4).
Close a group window	Double-click on its Control icon or press Ctrl+F4.
Close the Program Manager without cancelling printing	Click on its Minimize icon.
Collapse a branch	Press – or choose Collapse Branch.
Copy a program icon to another group	Press Ctrl and drag it.
Copy text	Select; then choose Copy from an Edit menu (or press Ctrl+Ins or Ctrl+C).
Copy files and directories on the same disk	Select; then Ctrl-drag, or press F8 and use the Copy command.
Copy files and directories onto a different disk	Select; then drag, or press F8 and use the Copy command.
Copy floppy disks	Choose Copy Disk from the File Manager's Disk menu.
Create a Help bookmark	Go to the topic and choose Bookmark from the Help menu.

To	Do
Create a new group	Choose New from the Program Manager's File menu; click Program Group; fill out a description and a command line.
Create a new directory	Click on the directory you want the new one to appear *under*, then choose Create Directory from the File Manager's File menu.
Cut text	Select; then choose Cut from an Edit menu (or press Shift+Del or Ctrl+X).
Delete a group	Click its icon an+ press Del.
Delete a file or directory	Select it; then choose Delete from the File menu.
Deselect all files	Press Ctrl+\.
Exit from the Program Manager	Double-click on its Control icon, or highlight Program Manager and click on End Task in the Task List, or press Alt+F4 when the Program Manager window is active.
Exit from Windows	Exit from the Program Manager.
Expand all the subdirectories of all of the directories	Press Ctrl+* or choose Expand All from the Tree menu.
Expand all the selected directory's subdirectories	Press * or choose Expand Branch from the Tree menu (File Manager).
Expand a selected directory one level (assuming it's got a - on it)	Press –, click on it, or choose Expand One Level from the Tree menu (File Manager).
Format floppy disks	Choose Format Disk from the File Manager's Disk menu.
Get help	Click on Help on the menu bar, press Alt+H, or press F1.
Go to DOS	Click on the DOS Prompt icon in the Main group.

To	Do
Go up one level	Click on [..]in a directory window (press Home to go directly to it).
Maximize a group window	Double-click on its title bar or click on its Maximize icon.
Maximize a window	Click on its Maximize icon or choose Maximize from its Control menu.
Minimize a window	Click on its Minimize icon or choose Minimize from its Control menu.
Move between group windows	Click in the one you want, or press Ctrl+F6 or Ctrl+Tab.
Move to another selection in the same window	Click or use the arrow keys.
Move files and directories	Select; then drag, or press F7 and use the Move on the same disk command.
Move a window	Drag it by its title bar or use the Control menu's Move command.
Move through a window	Drag or click in the scroll bars, or click on the arrow icons. In text windows, press PgUp or PgDn.
Move a program icon to another group	Drag it.
Move within a dialog box	Click in it, or press Tab to move forward or Shift+Tab to move backward.
Move files and directories onto a different disk	Select; then Alt-drag, or press F7 and use the Move command.
Open a document	Choose Open from a File menu (or press Alt-F and type O).
Open a new document	Choose New from a File menu (or press Alt-F and type N).
Open a directory folder	Double-click on its icon or press Enter when the icon is highlighted.

To	Do
Open a window	Double-click on its icon or press Enter when the icon is highlighted.
Paste	Select; then choose Paste from an Edit menu (or press Shif+Ins or Ctrl+V).
Pause the printer	Click Pause in the Print Manager window or press Alt+P.
Print files on the default printer	Select the document and choose Print from the File Manager's File menu or drag the document icon to the minimized Printer Manager.
Print a Windows document	Choose Print from the File menu to use the Windows Print Manager.
Print a non-Windows document	Use the print command in the program.
Rename a file or directory	Select it; then choose Rename from the File Manager's File menu.
Restore a window to its previous size	Click on its Restore icon or choose Restore from its Control menu.
Resume printing	Click Resume in the Print Manager window or press Alt+R.
Return to Windows from DOS	Type *exit* at the DOS prompt.
Run a program from the Program Manager	Double-click on its icon.
Save a document	Choose Save from a File menu (or press Alt+F and type S).
Save a new document	Choose Save As from a File menu (or press Alt+F and type A).
Scroll a list dialog box	Click on the up or down arrow in the scroll box, or type Alt-*letter* and then press the down arrow key.
Search for a file	Select Search from the File Manager's File menu.

To	Do
Search for a file by date	Select Sort by Date from the File Manager's View menu.
See what's on the Clipboard	Double-click on the Clipboard icon in the Main group.
Select the first file in a directory window	Press Home.
Select the last file in a directory window	Press End.
Select a file or directory	Click on it, or type the first letter of its name.
Select from menus	Click on the item or press Alt and type the underlined letter or number. When the pull-down menu appears, click on the item, or type the underlined letter or number. You can also highlight the name with the arrow keys and press Enter.
Select all files	Press Ctrl-/.
Select nonadjacent files directories	Ctrl-click.
Select adjacent files and directories	Shift-click, or use Shift and the arrow keys.
Shrink a group window to an icon	Double-click on its Control menu or click on its Minimize icon.
Size a window	Drag it outward or inward by its corner, or use the Control menu's Size command.
Start a program	Double-click on its icon, or choose Run from the Program Manager's or File Manager's File menu, or double-click on the DOS Prompt icon and use DOS, or press Enter when the icon is highlighted.
Start a program from the File Manager	Double-click on its icon, or use the Run command, or drag a document icon on top of its program file icon or a minimized program icon, or double-click on an associated document icon.

To	Do
Start a new document	Choose New from a File menu (or press Alt+F and type N).
Start Windows	Type *win* at the DOS prompt.
Stop printing a job or remove a job from the queue	Click Delete or press Alt+D in the Print Manager.
Switch to a different program that's running	Press Alt+Tab or Alt+Esc.
Switch to a different window	Click in it, or double-click on its name in the Task List, or press Alt+Tab to swtich to the Program Manager and open another window there.
Quit Windows	Double-click on the Program Manager's Control icon, or highlight Program Manager and click on End Task in the Task List, or press Alt+F4 when the Program Manager window is active.
Tile directory windows	Press Shift+F4 or pickTile from the Window menu.
Tile windows	Choose Tile from the Windows menu or press Shift+F4.
Undo what you just did	Choose Undo from an Edit menu (or press Alt+Backspace).
Use wildcards	The * stands for any combination of characters, and ? stands for any one character.

Shortcuts

To	Use
General	
Get the help Contents	F1
Open a file	Enter
Bring up the Task List	Ctrl+Esc
Cascade windows	Shift+F5
Tile windows	Shift+F4
Move to another selection in the same window	Arrow keys
Choose highlighted item from a menu	Enter
Cancel a menu	Esc
Move between menus	Arrow keys
Open and close a Control menu	Alt+Space bar; Alt+Hyphen
Switch to the next open program	Alt+Esc
Switch to the next open program, restoring minimized programs	Alt+Tab
Toggle between full-screen and windowed sizes	Alt+Enter
Exit Windows (when Program Manager is active)	Alt+F4

To	Use
In a document	
Copy	Ctrl+Ins
Cut	Shift+Del
Paste	Shift+Ins
Delete	Del
Move to the next or previous line	Down arrow or Up arrow
Move to the next or previous word	Ctrl+Right arrow or Ctrl+Left arrow
Move to the end or beginning of a line	End or Home
Move to the end or beginning of the document	Ctrl+End or Ctrl+Home
Move to the next or previous screen	PgDn or PgUp
Undo what you just did	Alt+Backspace
In a dialog box	
Move between selections	Tab or Shift+Tab
Move to a selection	Alt plus underlined letter
Move to the first or last item	Home or End
Open a drop-down list box	Alt-Down arrow
Select an item in a list box	Space bar
Select a check box	Space bar
Select all items in a list box	Ctrl-/
Select a command button	Enter
Close the box without selecting	Esc or Alt-F4

To	Use
To extend a selection	
To the next or previous line	Shift+Down arrow or Shift+Up arrow
To the end or beginning of the line	Shift+End or Shift+Home
Down or up one window	Shift+End or Shift+Home
Down or up one window	Shift+PgDn or Shift+PgUp
To the next or previous word	Ctrl+Shift+Right arrow or Ctrl+Shift+Left arrow
To the end or beginning of the document	Ctrl+Shift+End or Ctrl+Shift+Home
In the Program Manager	
Get help on the Program Manager	Alt+H or F1
Move between group windows	Ctrl+F6 or Ctrl+Tab
Start a highlighted icon	Enter
Close a group window	Ctrl+F4
Exit from the Program Manager (Windows)	Alt+F4
In the File Manager	
Get help on the File Manager	Alt+H or F1
Open a directory	Enter
Expand a collapsed directory one level	+
Expand all the selected directory's subdirectories	*

To	Use
Expand all the subdirectories of all of the directories	Ctrl+*
Collapse a directory	– (hyphen)
Move a file or directory	F7
Copy a file or directory	F8
Select a file	Type the first letter of its name
Select the first file in the window	Home
Select the last file in the window	End
Select all files in a window	Ctrl+/
Deselect all files	Ctrl-+\

Index

386 computer, 1
386 Enhanced control panel, 82, 92

A

Accessories group, 4, 40
adding fonts, 102-104, 107
adding printers, 98-100, 107
Adobe Type Manager, 104
Alt+Backspace, for Undo, 31, 37
Alt+Esc, to cycle among windows, 19
Alt+Tab, to switch between programs, 19
annotating Help topics, 93-94
application windows, 18
applications, setting up, 46-47, 49
Applications group, 9
arranging icons, 22
arrowheads, to indicate pop-up lists, 17
associating documents with programs, 72-73, 78
AUTOEXEC.BAT, changing your, 109

B

beep, responding to, 111
bitmapped fonts, 101, 104

bookmarks, using in Help, 93
borders, dragging windows by, 4
branches, expanding and collapsing, 58-60, 77
browsing, to locate directories, 27
bus mouse, 110

C

Calculator, 4
Calendar, 4
canceling a dialog box, 15
canceling printing, 96, 107
capacities, of floppy disks, 75
cascading windows, 20-21, 23, 77
CD-ROM drives, 93
changing group names, 47, 49
changing icons, 46, 49
changing screen colors, 82-85, 94
Character Map, 40
characters in file names, 52
check boxes, using, 16
clicking, 3
Clipboard, using the, 31-33
Clipboard viewer, 9
closing a window, 7, 18, 23
.CLP, as Clipboard extension, 33

collapsing and expanding branches, 58-60, 77
color palette, 83-84
color refiner cursor, 85
Color control panel, 81, 82-85
colors, changing screen, 82-85
COM ports, and mouse, 110
COM1, 92
command buttons, 17
Control menu, using, 6, 18, 19, 32
Control Panel, 9, 81-93
copying text and graphics, 31-32, 37
copying and moving icons, 45, 49
copying directories, 64-65, 78
copying disks, 74, 79
copying files, 64-65, 78
copying, in non-Windows programs, 112
copying the screen, 32, 33, 37
creating directories, 66, 78
creating subdirectories, 67
Ctrl+Alt+Del, 111
Ctrl+C, to copy, 32, 37
Ctrl+Esc, to display Task List, 19, 23
Ctrl+Ins, to copy, 32, 37
Ctrl+V, to paste, 32, 27
Ctrl+X, to cut, 32, 37
Ctrl+Z, for Undo, 31,37

V

This Little Windows Book, 3.1 edition, was
edited in Microsoft Word.
Grayscale screen shots were taken in Tiffany
Plus. Text and graphics were sent via a
Sitka/TOPS network to my
Macintosh II running System 7, where
page makeup was done in Aldus Pagemaker
(thank you, Matt Kim).
The book's design, which includes custom
Little Book Fonts as well as ITC New
Baskerville and Futura Book, is by
Olav Martin Kvern,
based on an original design by
Robin Williams.

More from Peachpit Press. . .

DeskJet Unlimited, 2nd Edition
Steve Cummings
An in-depth guide to the HP DeskJet family of printers, including information on fonts, troubleshooting, and DeskJet programming. *(393 pages)*

Desktop Publishing Secrets
Robert Eckhardt, Bob Weibel, and Ted Nace
Hundreds of the best desktop publishing tips from 5 years of *Publish* magazine. *(550 pages)*

The LaserJet Font Book
Katherine Pfeiffer
A buyer's guide to LaserJet fonts and a tutorial on using type effectively. Shows hundreds of LaserJet fonts from over a dozen vendors. *(320 pages)*

LaserJet IIP Essentials
Steve Cummings, Mike Handa, and Jerold Whitmore
Covers configuration and use of the IIP with major word processing, database, spreadsheet, and desktop publishing programs. *(340 pages)*

Letter to a Computer Novice
Larry Magid
An introduction to personal computers that assumes no prior technical knowledge. *(160 pages, available Spring 1992)*

The Little DOS 5 Book
Kay Yarborough Nelson
A quick and accessible guide to DOS 5. Includes numerous tips, tricks, and charts of keyboard shortcuts. *(160 pages)*

The Little Laptop Book
Steve Cummings
Provides information on using applications and utilities, printing on the road, and telecommunication. *(192 pages)*

The Little WordPerfect Book
Skye Lininger
Gives step-by-step instructions for setting page margins, typing text, navigating with the cursor keys, and more. *(160 pages)*

The Little WordPerfect for Windows Book
Kay Yarborough Nelson
A quick and accessible guide to WordPerfect for Windows. Includes numerous tips and charts of keyboard shortcuts. *(200 pages)*

Mastering Corel Draw, 2nd Edition
Chris Dickman and Rick Altman
Provides beginning lessons and advanced tips on using this remarkable drawing program for Windows. Includes disk. *(408 pages)*

PageMaker 4: An Easy Desk Reference
Robin Williams
A reference book that lets you look up how to do specific tasks with PageMaker 4. 0. *(784 pages, available Spring 1992)*

PageMaker 4: Visual QuickStart Guide
Webster and Associates
Provides a highly visual introduction to desktop publishing in PageMaker 4.0 for the PC. *(176 pages)*

The PC is not a typewriter
Robin Williams
Explains the principles behind the techniques for professional typesetting and how they can be utilized on the desktop. *(96 pages)*

Ventura Tips and Tricks, 3rd Edition
Ted Nace and Daniel Will-Harris
Performance tips, advice on using Ventura utilities, useful tables and charts, and clear explanations. *(790 pages)*

Winning! The Awesome & Amazing Book of Windows Game Tips, Traps, & Sneaky Tricks
John Hedtke
This book provides rules and explanations for setting up, running, and mastering each game in the Microsoft Entertainment Packs. *(232 pages)*

WordPerfect: Desktop Publishing in Style, 2nd Edition
Daniel Will-Harris
Peachpit's popular guide to producing documents with WordPerfect 5.1 or 5.0. *(650 pages)*

Order Form
(800) 283-9444 or (510) 548-4393
(510) 548-5991 fax

#	Title	Price	Total
	DeskJet Unlimited, 2nd Edition	23.95	
	Desktop Publishing Secrets	27.95	
	The LaserJet Font Book	24.95	
	LaserJet IIP Essentials	21.95	
	Letter to a Computer Novice (available Spring 1992)	12.95	
	The Little DOS 5 Book	12.95	
	The Little Laptop Book	14.95	
	The Little Windows Book, 3.1 Edition	12.95	
	The Little WordPerfect Book	12.95	
	The Little WordPerfect for Windows Book	12.95	
	Mastering Corel Draw, 2nd Edition (with disk)	32.95	
	PageMaker 4: An Easy Desk Reference (PC Edition)	29.95	
	PageMaker 4: Visual QuickStart Guide (PC Edition)	12.95	
	The PC is not a typewriter	9.95	
	Ventura Tips and Tricks, 3rd Edition	27.95	
	Winning! The Awesome and Amazing Book of Windows Game Tips, Traps, and Sneaky Tricks	14.95	
	WordPerfect: Desktop Publishing in Style, 2nd Edition	23.95	

Tax of 8.25% applies to California residents only. UPS ground shipping: $4 for first item, $1 each additional. UPS 2nd day air: $7 for first item, $2 each additional. Air mail to Canada: $6 for first item, $4 each additional. Air mail overseas: $14 each item.	Subtotal	
	8.25% Tax (CA only)	
	Shipping	
	TOTAL	

Name

Company

Address

City   State   Zip

Phone   Fax

❏ Check enclosed   ❏ Visa   ❏ MasterCard

Company purchase order #

Credit card #   Expiration Date

Peachpit Press, Inc. • 2414 Sixth Street • Berkeley, CA • 94710
Your satisfaction is guaranteed or your money will be cheerfully refunded!